SEARCHING

for

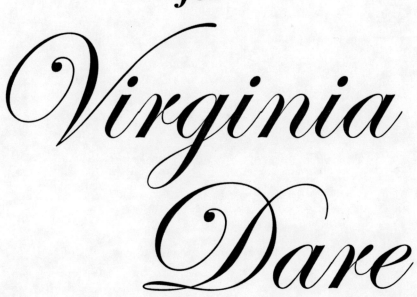

Virginia Dare

SEARCHING

for

Virginia Dare

MARJORIE HUDSON

PRESS53
LEWISVILLE, NC

Press53

Suite 202
6610 Shallowford Road
Lewisville, NC 27023

FIRST EDITION

Book design by Kevin Watson
Cover art, "Morning Light," by John Sagartz
Map design by Stacye Leanza

Grateful acknowledgment is made to the following for permission to excerpt their work:

To Henry Taylor, for excerpt from "Understanding Fiction," a poem first
published in *The Sewanee Review*, Winter 1996. Copyright © 1996 by Henry
Taylor. Now the title poem in *Understanding Fiction, Poems 1986-1996*,
published by Louisiana State University Press.

To the North Carolina Collection, University of North Carolina Library at
Chapel Hill, for excerpts from John White's maps of Roanoke Island and
vicinity (compass rose and map edge detail). Engraving by Theodor de Bry.

To Charles Baxter, for excerpt from *The Feast of Love* copyright © 2001 by
Charles Baxter. Published by Vintage Contemporaries.

Printed on acid-free paper
ISBN: 978-0-9793049-6-5

For my parents
And all who came before us

I have long ago decided that all our boasted knowledge is as nothing compared to what we do not know, and all new discoveries possibly tame to what lies buried in the past.

—Sallie Southall Cotten,
on speculation that Eden
is located in the Yucatan

But I tell it again, and see how

*To help you believe it, so I make
Some adjustment of voice or detail,
And the story strides into the future.*

—Henry Taylor,
"Understanding Fiction"

Contents

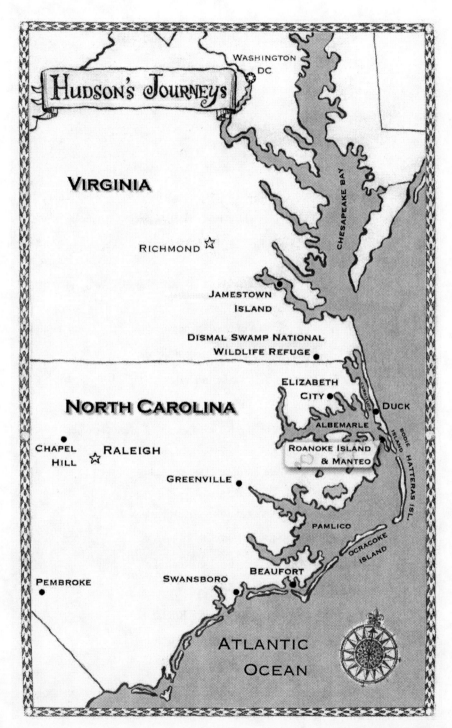

HUDSON'S JOURNEYS

WASHINGTON DC

VIRGINIA

RICHMOND

JAMESTOWN ISLAND

DISMAL SWAMP NATIONAL WILDLIFE REFUGE

CHESAPEAKE BAY

NORTH CAROLINA

ELIZABETH CITY

DUCK

ALBEMARLE

CHAPEL HILL

RALEIGH

ROANOKE ISLAND & MANTEO

BODIE ISLAND

HATTERAS ISL.

GREENVILLE

PAMLICO

OCRACOKE ISLAND

PEMBROKE

SWANSBORO

BEAUFORT

ATLANTIC OCEAN

Timeline of Significant Events

1500s

1524   Verrazzano explores NC coast.

1540   DeSoto visits Cheraw territory.

1583   Sir Humphrey Gilbert colony at Newfoundland fails.

1584   *March.* Queen Elizabeth grants New World lands to Raleigh.

             April. Philip Amadas and Arthur Barlowe scout Roanoke Island.

1585   *April.* Ralph Lane brings 100 soldiers to Roanoke; White and Hariot document findings.

             September. Grenville and others depart Roanoke for England, for resupply.

1586   *June 19.* Ralph Lane's expedition leaves with Sir Francis Drake.

             July. Grenville returns; leaves 15 soldiers.

1587   *April 2.* Sir Francis Drake begins effort to sink 100+ Spanish ships.

             April 26. John White and colonists depart England.

             June 22. John White and his men catch "5 great tortoises" near St. Croix.

             July 22. John White lands at Hatteras, takes 40 men to Roanoke.

             July 23. White finds skeleton, huts at Roanoke.

             July 28. George Howe shot with 16 arrows.

             August 18. Virginia Dare born at Roanoke.

             August 24. Virginia Dare baptized.

             August 27. John White departs for England.

             October 9. Queen's moratorium on shipping.

             October 16. White arrives home.

             November. John White and Raleigh plan first Roanoke resupply mission.

1588	*Spring.* Spanish spy ship finds abandoned Roanoke colony.
	April 22. White departs on doomed Roanoke supply mission.
	July. Spanish Armada attacks England.
1589	Plans for Roanoke supply mission aborted.
1590	*March.* White departs on Roanoke supply mission; finds CROATOAN carving.
1593	*February.* White sends account of 1590 voyage to Richard Hakluyt for publication.
1599	Date marked on last Eleanor Dare Stone.

1600s

1600s	Powhatan claims to have slaughtered Roanoke colonists in early part of century.
1602	Raleigh sends a ship to search for colonists.
1603	Queen Elizabeth dies; King James succeeds to throne.
1606	*December 20.* Jamestown colonists set sail for New World.
1610	Jamestown secretary William Strachey records report of Roanoke survivors.
1617	Raleigh sets out for gold mine in Guiana.
1618	*November.* Raleigh beheaded.
1625 - 1750	Range of dates for stratum in which Kendall ring found at Croatoan.
1650	Approximate date of two Indian burials at Croatoan village.
1650	Date by which Adolph Dial says colonists/Croatoans may have settled in Robeson County.
1660	Morgan Jones captured in southeast NC by Indians who speak English.
1670	John Lederer visits the Chowanoc, Tuscarora, Cheraw, and Santee. Learns that "bearded men" live to the southwest.

1700s

1701	John Lawson views Roanoke fort ruins and reports gray-eyed Indians.

Chapter 1:

SEARCHING FOR VIRGINIA DARE

*I applied mine heart to know and to search, and to seek
out wisdom, and the reason of things...*
                                                —Ecclesiastes 7:25

LET'S SAY THERE'S A SCUPPERNONG VINE, *its trunk the size of an elephant's
leg—no, the size of a baobab tree. Its tendrils extend across miles and miles of
coastal drift, along sand and even into the water. Bronze globes float in the
brine when the tide is gentle, become crushed and pulpy in pounding storms.
Let's say it's August, and the Gulf Stream is warm, and it is bringing things
to shore that the shore has never seen: gold signet rings; Spanish amphoras
filled with wine; the bones of Englishmen. Let's say there's sex in this story,
and beautiful virgins, and the root of the vine goes deep beneath the sand to
the river of time. And the river of time connects all things, sifts and dissolves
all memories of scented vines, all bones, all intentions into one slow moving
tide of myth; we dip our feet in it. Myth is the language in which we live, that
soaks and permeates everything we know and most of what we don't know.*

———

THE COASTAL ISLANDS OF NORTH CAROLINA sweep up the mainland shore
like a string of long beads hugging the scalloped neckline of a dress,
from the South Carolina border to Bald Head at the mouth of the Cape
Fear, up past Wrightsville to a stretch of summer resort towns. North of
Cape Lookout, the Outer Banks scatter toward the Gulf Stream, as if
stretching to hold the vast waters of Pamlico Sound: here are the wilder

reaches of the coast, Portsmouth and Ocracoke, Hatteras and Pea Island. Here are more treacherous inlets and shifting sands. Just as the string returns to hug the mainland, there is an anomaly: Roanoke Island, doubled up behind Nags Head, straddling Albemarle and Pamlico Sounds—an extra bead strung between the Banks and the main. The single strand continues, past Albemarle Sound, up Currituck to peter out at Back Bay, beyond the Virginia border.

The sand banks shift and twist with the winds of nor'easters and hurricanes; the sounds behind them swell with fresh water in flood, invade rivers and inlets in high salty tides. Betwixt and between, Roanoke Island bides her time, anchored by bridges, awash and protected in the amniotic fluid of two great estuaries. On this island, among shifting tides and treacherous bars, England made her first American colony. She staked her tenuous claim on the New World with the birth of a girl child, baptized Virginia Dare. What happened to that girl child is one of America's great mysteries:

> *An English baby is born in an island wilderness.*
> *The baby and her family and friends all disappear.*
> *They leave behind two cryptic messages carved in trees: CRO*
> *and CROATOAN.*
> *No one knows where they went.*
> *Or whether they survived.*

Speculation on the fate of the colony has grown over four centuries like a grapevine planted in fertile soil, sending off tendrils in all directions, having long since wrapped the facts of the story in extravagant ornament.

In 1999 I set out on a fool's errand, in search of Virginia Dare. Like a toddler wandering off in a snowstorm, Virginia and her Lost Colony have compelled many failed searches. They have inspired books filled with bizarre theories, obscure studies, legends, and even an epic poem whose heroine is blonde with misty blue eyes and a pink-beribboned bonnet. I found myself browsing the back shelves of university historical collections, cracking bindings on books that had not been opened in fifty years. At first Virginia's story seemed dusty and unused as some of those books. But as I dug deeper I felt the irresistible pull of some deep new story, fresh territory for someone like me who wasn't born in North Carolina, someone who came from the north to settle here: *You mean there was a colony before Jamestown? Before Plymouth? How come I never heard of it?*

The more I found out about Virginia Dare, the more I found myself seduced by her: She seems to captivate those bent on obsession. She brings out the storytellers and mythmakers and charlatans, people who pick a single aspect of her story and let it fester in their minds, for reasons that may have very little to do with the facts. The facts are thin branches on which they hang elaborations. There is a grandfather, a daughter, and a babe. All are lost. Much of the rest is context or conjecture.

I soon learned the meaning behind something people say here in the South: *I know what happened to Virginia Dare.* They mean they know a story, and you'd better listen, because it's a good one and it's been kept secret for a long, long time.

There are times in everyone's life when a good story is what you need. A story full of hope and tragic endings, speculation and drama, a story that binds you more tightly to your life, your family, your hopes, when it seems these things might spin out of reach. Or a story that spins you into a new world before you have a chance to take a breath and say, Stop. The summer of 1999 was one of those times for me. And the story I found did both – cleaved me more tightly to my life, and opened up a world.

I started out thinking facts would satisfy me. The facts are extraordinary in themselves, making a shape like an Elizabethan drama wrapped in deerskin. Virginia Dare was the first child born of English parents on American soil, on August 18, 1587. She was part of the first English attempt to plant families in the New World, a colony of one hundred-plus sturdy souls. The expedition was governed by her grandfather, John White; organized by Sir Walter Raleigh; and had the blessing of Queen Elizabeth. Virginia survived long enough to be baptized. She was likely still alive when John White shipped back to England for supplies. And, as people around here like to say, *she was never seen again by European eyes.*

The colonists arrived in the midst of hurricane season. It was also one of the worst drought periods in 800 years. Most of the local tribes— Roanoke and Hattorask on the banks, Chesepiuk and Chowanoc on the mainland—weren't feeling very friendly, and they were hard up for food.

These were not the first English to make it to Roanoke Island, and they were not the only ones to get lost. In fact, if you count a boatload of slaves, reports of a shipwreck, and several explorers left behind in the woods, the population of lost and abandoned people at Roanoke by the time Virginia Dare showed up may have counted well over four hundred.

This colony brought seventeen women to Roanoke Island; one gave birth shortly after Virginia was born, and one came with a babe in arms. There were eleven boys on the ship's roster. There were eighty-five men. They had come for the promise of 500 acres each. They were hoping to find silver and gold. They intended to build America's first English city, the Cittie of Raleigh, on the shores of the Chesapeake Bay.

In short, they had come with the idea of raising children and improving their fortunes—and they had come to the wrong place.

SPECULATION ABOUT THE LIFE OF VIRGINIA DARE spins and glimmers at the nucleus of the mystery of the Lost Colony. The life of Eleanor Dare, her mother, spins in close proximity. Politicians and poets once portrayed Eleanor as the "first mother" of America and Virginia as the "first daughter." Scholars attach the charged particles of Indian politics and Elizabethan economies. Writers engage in personality studies of characters such as Raleigh, who has been called, in my hearing, "the most hated and feared Englishman of his time" and "a clever poet"—among other things. At least one sculptor has portrayed Virginia in the form of a Greek goddess. Folklorists spin out ghosty stories like swamp mist, and archeologists still sift through dirt and midden for physical evidence of her fate.

I saw right away that the story of Virginia Dare is a family story. A child is born; a mother is caught in an Indian war; a father protects them as best he can; and a grandfather—grumpy, desperate, and bumbling—spends years trying to save them, butting his head against obstacles such as hurricanes, Queen Elizabeth, and the Spanish Armada.

One family record remains: John White's journal. While detailing every turn of the 1587 voyage, Governor White says little about his daughter or granddaughter other than recording the birth and baptism of Virginia, and praising God for their safe arrival. Perhaps he felt it proper to record these things with restraint; perhaps his mind was occupied with the weight of all his troubles. Still, White was a father and grandfather on a dangerous mission, and his journals of 1587 and later years all have a tone of desperation. His sympathies seem to be with women—settler and Native alike. He notes dangers Englishwomen encounter at every turn; he devotes hours to recording the figures of women and children in Native villages.

White had explored and documented Roanoke Island on at least one earlier expedition and had intimate knowledge of the territory. He knew it was not suited for settlement. His accounts of later rescue attempts are full of financial frustrations, bad storms, incompetent captains, and disastrous tangents into piracy. He seems gripped in a species of madness, to continue to dream of the success of the colony while his own kin are in peril for their lives.

As the first official illustrator of the New World, White was and still is known for his depictions of Native people and villages, wilderness plants and animals—an astonishing wealth of images brought back to England in 1586. But he made no drawings of his later voyages; many of his books and papers were lost, so we can't know all he wrote. Still, White survived for years after his colonists went missing; he could have written accounts from memory or attempted to redraw some of his lost paintings.

If John White ever sketched his granddaughter, no record remains. For a grandfather who was an artist by profession, that's tantamount to throwing away the camera the day your first grandchild is born.

What was the family story? White's first child, a son, was dead. His wife may have died bearing Eleanor; she did not accompany him to the New World. White may have brought a brother or other relation to Roanoke in addition to his son-in-law, Ananias, daughter Eleanor, and granddaughter Virginia. After several failed attempts at rescue, White gave up. He kept publishing accounts of his failures, perhaps for posterity, more likely for cash. Can you imagine writing the story of how you lost your family in the wilds of America, and how it was your fault? He posted one last account to his publisher in 1593 and remained silent ever after on the subject of his own griefs and motivations.

There is much more to Virginia's story than family, of course. There is the complex web of Elizabethan politics, piracy, and warfare; there is the spy network of Spain. There are treasure ships, and slave ships, and warring tribes of Native Americans; there is murder and kidnapping and plague. Bizarre, appealing legends circulate of the colony's survival among the Indians, in the swamps, and as far away as Florida. The images in these stories are compelling: a baby born; a mother, abandoned in the wilderness; the disappearance, wholly and utterly, of the colonists; the words carved in trees—that partial word, CRO, as if a hand was stopped, mid-stroke. In this story are gold and pearls, Indians canoeing in the Thames, an enormous grapevine that grows where the colonists lived. A white doe haunts the shores of Albemarle Sound, a doe that used to be Virginia Dare.

Virginia is a blank slate people draw upon. We have long since made up for John White's silence.

Traveling the legendary path of the colonists, and looking into the mystery that is Virginia Dare, set my mind on a parallel journey—an exploration of my own family story and the myths that govern my own life. Why does Virginia's story haunt me? Perhaps because, like my own, it is marked by loss and blank pages the imagination loves to fill.

MY MOTHER AND FATHER LIVED THROUGH THE GREAT DEPRESSION, the Second World War, the sixties, and my rocky adolescence, in that order. I have imagined my mother, the social worker, sitting in front of a glowing radio in a dusky room, listening to the news of Pearl Harbor. I have imagined my father standing before his draft board, proving he's a pacifist, in December 1941. I imagined these things because they didn't talk about them. What they did talk about came out in bits and spurts—one-line assessments that hinted at who they once were. My father tells the story of his youth:

> *My father died when I was five.*
> *I got a paper route.*
> *Mother took in boarders.*
> *Bob and I slept on the back porch in winter.*
> *One day we woke up covered in snow.*

I love those few bright details to frame the mystery of my father's life: death; mother; snow. In them is a beginning, a window to the mystery that is my family. In recent years I have been asking my parents for stories of their lives. More and more they have obliged me. I have learned snippets of tales that chill my bones, things that are concealed from children. Again, my father, the preacher:

> *There was a lady in the church who had hallucinations.*
> *She thought your mother was controlling her mind.*
> *She came with a gun late one night and shot the church.*

Our parsonage was just yards from that church. But all I remember of that time is being whisked away for a stay with Grandmother Swanson, who had a cat named Bootsie, a black cat with little white paws.

Gaps in the stories still dominate my understanding of things; the mind moves like water to fill empty places.

In August of 1999, in the midst of my first months of research on the Lost Colony, I attended a 100th birthday memorial for my grandmother Rapp, born in 1899, dead for seven years. Three months later, my husband Sam's grandmother Hudson died. She was ninety-nine. Both women lived for most of the twentieth century. What stories they could have told. But they didn't—not much, anyway, to me. In the aftermath of these deaths, I craved family stories: keys to unlock the mystery of our lives.

SKINNER FUNERAL HOME, DUNN, N.C. NOVEMBER 17, 1999. The casket is open, and to my amazement she is beautiful, like Sleeping Beauty banked in summer flowers. She is wearing her customary eyeglasses and aqua velour robe. People stand and stare, then move away to visit with the living. I ask a cousin to tell a family story, preferably one about my husband Sam's dad, a preacher's kid. I like P.K. stories, because I'm one myself (those preachers' kids are *wild*). Next thing I know, we're laughing doubled over at the image of young Daddy up on the roof, smoking cigarettes, the Reverend throwing rocks at him to make him come down. We have almost forgotten that death is in the room.

Suddenly it's just me laughing, my loud Yankee voice reverbing against the walls and windowpanes. I turn around. "It's time for silent prayer," someone stage-whispers; just like that, we all bow our heads, close our eyes, and seal our lips.

At graveside, a daughter reads a tribute:

> *Mrs. Hudson was a schoolteacher.*
> *She lived in Red Springs.*
> *On her honeymoon, she went to the Louisville zoo but she didn't look at a single animal.*
> *She spent the whole time sitting on the bench rubbing her feet.*
> *She had worn fancy new shoes.*

EVEN AT A FUNERAL YOU CAN GET THE STORY WRONG. The image of Daddy smoking on the roof is what I remember—but it's not what really happened.

Chapter 2:

Stepping into the New World

"We are as near to heaven by sea as by land."
—last words of Sir Humphrey Gilbert,
first English colonist in America and Sir
Walter Raleigh's half brother

*"The second of July, we found shole water, which smelt
so sweetly, and was so strong a smell, as if we had bene
in the midst of some delicate garden..."*
—from Arthur Barlowe's first encounter
with the New World

PORTSMOUTH, ENGLAND. APRIL 26, 1587. Three English ships set sail this day for the New World. They comprise the third of Raleigh's missions to America, his second attempt at a colony, the first to include women and children.

The names "Eleanor Dare" and "John White" trip off the tongues of native Carolinians, but the rest of the country never heard of these people whose spectacular courage built a foundation for the Jamestown colony. Their story seems a shameful failure to some, a flag of courage to others, and a secret to the rest of us. I keep wondering, *Who were those people? Why would they take such risks?* There's a lot left out of the history books.

I can't help but think what an astounding thing it was for a parent to do: willingly walk the gangplank to an English ship and—for the first time in history—trust their bodies and souls and children to the Atlantic for four months, then to the unknown wilderness of the New World.

Edenic and fruitful by reputation, Virginia (which included all lands claimed by the English between Florida and Cape Breton) was also full of dangerous beasts, rotten weather, and riled Indians—and John White knew it, from at least one previous voyage.

From what we know of them, the colonists were not desperate or foolish people. They were neither indentured servants nor lords and ladies; they were members of guilds and solid citizens. Perhaps they were inspired by John White's paintings, or Sir Walter's poetry, or the seductive claims of explorers. Each of twelve "assistants," or leaders, for the venture recruited a small group of prospective settlers—most likely citizens who had some personal loyalty or guild or family connection. Perhaps the opportunity to be the first colonists was presented to them like an insider stock trade or a new IPO—take a risk now, make a fast fortune. They may not have known that the reason they would be "first" was that others had failed.

The colonists were no doubt devout; perhaps they trusted in God, not Sir Walter. Perhaps they were persuaded by their governor, John White, an artist by trade, whose prime credential for leadership seems to have been his love and knowledge of the New World as reflected in his drawings. The settlers would have many opportunities on their voyage to use the new *Book of Common Prayer*, in which were compiled handy supplications on a variety of topics: deliverance from lightning and tempest; rescue from plague, pestilence, and famine; help for women in childbirth.

The colonists left behind a country in the throes of the Renaissance, a period when science and art were beginning to clash with religion. In a few years Shakespeare's prolific outpouring of plays would invade the Rose Theater. The plague still claimed lives on a regular basis in rat-infested London. Spain dominated the New World, enslaving and converting its people with equal zeal, and ransacking its cities of gold. To Queen Elizabeth's great chagrin, the Atlantic swarmed with Spanish treasure ships and rumors abounded of a great armada assembling to attack England.

I begin to understand why the colonists might want to leave England. But why come to this strange place, full of peril?

To answer this question, I must go back to the beginning of the story.

PORTSMOUTH, ENGLAND, APRIL 27, 1584. *We departed the west of England with two barkes, well furnished with men and victuals...* [1] Thus begins the account of Arthur Barlowe's voyage to the New World, the first of the Roanoke voyages. I've been haunting the University of North Carolina-Chapel Hill's historical collection for weeks, sitting in a red leather chair in Wilson Rounds Library, digging into a polished oak card catalog, filling out small slips of paper to request books that haven't been taken out since the 1950s.

In 1589, Richard Hakluyt published a compilation of reports of all three expeditions to Roanoke Island in *Hakluyt's Voyages of the English*. In 1955, the granddaddy of Roanoke Colony research, David Beers Quinn, compiled and published relevant excerpts from Hakluyt's *Voyages*, English court records and letters, ships' logs, and Spanish court records in a handy two-volume set, now published in paperback: *The Roanoke Voyages*. Printed with maps and references, in this compilation lies almost all the documentary clues there are to how Virginia Dare's mother made it to the New World, and what awaited her there. Quinn notes that some valuable materials, including White's early papers and Hariot's accounts of the first voyage, were never published and have either been lost forever or await discovery in some dusty library. Who knows? Maybe someday they will come to light.

THE STORY OF THE THREE ROANOKE VOYAGES starts with one man: Sir Walter Raleigh. In the English court of the early 1580s, Sir Walter was the queen's darling. When he was not planning colonies or invading Ireland, he was tripping through the palace on pearl-encrusted slippers, writing odes to the queen's beauty and wit. In addition to being a dandy, Raleigh was a true Renaissance man with a deep interest in science, nature, and exploration. He enjoyed the powerful yet frustrating position of being the queen's chief entertainer and friend without much say in policy—and without permission to venture from her side as far as the New World.

Elizabeth did, however, grant him this tantalizing prize: the right to all the lands of North America as yet unclaimed by Spain—as long as he colonized them within six years. By 1570 Spain already had ten outposts in the area that is now Florida, Georgia, and South Carolina and was exploring the North Carolina and Virginia coasts. Elizabeth was determined to halt its progress in North America. Raleigh would claim these lands with his hundred-odd settlers or "planters." Their lives would stake his fortune, but he himself was forbidden to go.

Implicit in the queen's gift to Raleigh was the chance of finding gold and precious minerals, either in the kingdoms of the New World or on Spanish ships that would unsuspectingly float northward past the English outpost on their way home. Shipping took this predictable route in the Atlantic, based on prevailing winds and currents. If halting Spain's progress in taking over the New World was a major motive for planting an English colony, finding gold was another.

England had gone after gold and land before in the New World: In 1576, an effort to find a Northwest passage had led to a fool's gold rush when the ship brought back a rock from Newfoundland that had a promising gleam. With the queen's backing, a team of miners and colonists set out, got lost, came home, and learned that assayists had determined their "gold" was just a yellow rock. In 1583, Raleigh's half brother, Sir Humphrey Gilbert, had obtained the queen's patent to colonize Newfoundland, but failed miserably. He went down with his ship.

The queen, not wanting to squander her own resources on such precarious doings, now dangled the golden carrot to Raleigh. In March 1584 she transferred Gilbert's license to him and his heirs "for ever hereafter to discover search fynde out and viewe such remote heathen and barbarous landes Contries and territories not actually possessed of any Christian Prynce and inhabited by Christian people. . . ."[2]

Raleigh's patent extended to "all Cittyes Castles townes villages and places" in those lands, but the Crown reserved the right to keep one fifth of any gold or silver found. The Virgin Queen gave Raleigh virtually all of North America excluding Florida, which was claimed by Spain. Later she would grant the great privilege of naming his lands "Virginia" in her honor. The language of the patent granted to Raleigh spins a vision of great wealth: gold for the treasury; luminous castles; great cities. Some of that gold might come from English raids on unsuspecting Spanish treasure ships. Someone had to stop Spain from taking over the entire New World.

To plant an English fort and colony was the key, and the first step would be to find a suitable location.

Raleigh moved fast to fulfill his end of the bargain. In April 1584, just over a month later, he sent Philip Amadas and Arthur Barlowe with two ships to the New World to explore the coast and find a site for a colony. It would be the first of three efforts toward colonization under Raleigh's patent. By July 2, the company was approaching the Outer Banks and encountered "[shoal] water, which smelt so sweetly, and was so strong a smell, as if we had bene in the midst of some delicate garden. . . ."[3]

Barlowe described

many goodly woods, full of Deere, Conies, Hares, and Fowle . . . in incredible abundance,[4]

not to mention

the reddest Cedars of the world,[5]

and sandy shores that were

so full of grapes, as the very beating, and surge of the Sea ouerflowed them.[6]

Barlowe found the coastal inhabitants friendly and pleasant and their world like a small paradise. He learned that Europeans had been there before. The Natives spoke of a shipwreck, and showed tools made of salvaged spikes. They also spoke of white men, castaways, living to the west, who twenty-six years before had strapped two canoes together, put their shirts up on masts, and sailed away, never to be seen again.

Barlowe left with knowledge of a seemingly ideal secret port for privateering: Roanoke Island, hidden away behind the first stretch of banks, protected from Spanish ships by shoal waters and sandbars. The only "gold" he found was the gleaming metal disks, probably copper, worn by the chiefs. But where copper lies, silver is often found. Barlowe was not discouraged.

Barlowe brought back two Indian allies, Wanchese and Manteo, who would provide much useful information about their language and culture to English admirers and future voyagers. Wanchese's visit to England may have soured him on the foreigners; on his return, he became an enemy to English settlers. On Manteo, however, the English and her queen must have made a great impression. Through much later strife and toil, Manteo stayed unaccountably loyal to Raleigh's people.

Barlowe also brought back the only recorded joke about the colonists, repeated later by Raleigh in his *History of the World*. When the English asked the Croatoans the name of their country, the Croatoans could only say "Wingandacon," which, not knowing the Native language, the English assumed was the answer to their question. But what the Natives were saying was "what nice clothes you wear" – this from a people who wore scant coverings but intricate decorations, including an entire bird in the headdress of a holy man, and ropes and earrings and bracelets of pearls. (One can only imagine what they'd say if they saw Raleigh's pearl-encrusted slippers.) The English misuse of the word doubtless provoked laughs around the Natives' campfires. Ever after, to them, the English would be "men who wear clothes."

Confusion about place names dogged the English; they got it wrong from the beginning. "Croatoan" they used to refer to Manteo's people and their village. It more likely meant the expanse of hunting territory those people claimed, including several islands and portions of the mainland. "Hatteras" or "Hattorask" is what the English called the island; it was the tribal name.

———

IN APRIL 1585, RALEIGH SENT HIS SECOND VENTURE TO ROANOKE, a colony of 100 soldiers under Ralph Lane. By then English relations with Spain had become outright hostile. The hostilities threatened the queen's sea trade but also gave a English captains a good excuse to seize Spanish frigates laden with gold. In addition to seeking a safe place for settlers, Lane's men would outfit Roanoke as an outpost for English privateering. But the great treasure yielded by this second venture would not be silver and gold; it would be the journals, maps, and drawings of two colleagues on the voyage—Thomas Hariot and John White.

Throughout the sounds and bays of East Carolina, White documented flora and fauna, culture and people, in watercolors that still provide a rare glimpse into the pre-colonial Native American world. White and Hariot apparently enjoyed their work immensely, traveling by boat and by foot to villages as far away as the Chesapeake Bay, communicating with the Natives as well as they could, smoking tobacco and feasting, and noticing that their status was more that of gods than men. Where White detailed the people and plants, swallowtail butterflies and fish in his drawings, Hariot transcribed the lay of the land. With White, he made such accurate maps of the coast of North America that some portions can be compared to today's satellite images. Hariot also provided the science, by collecting plants and animals, testing minerals, studying the stars.

Hariot's journal includes analysis of the religious and social practices of Natives. "The whole country," Hariot reports, treated the Englishmen with "wonderful admiration." He goes on to explain that the Natives noticed the English had the power to strike them dead from afar if they dealt the English "wicked practices." Villagers were falling by the score to mysterious illnesses, even in places where the English had long since moved on.[7] English guns were impressive, almost magical weapons. And because there were no women on the expedition, some Natives believed the English might be immortal—not of woman born.[8]

Hariot and White were learning much about the ways of the New World. They discovered that the changeable shoals and inlets along the Outer Banks would make Roanoke an unsuitable site for a colony. On a trip up to Chesepiuk Indian territory, White found a friendly village that would welcome English planters. Perhaps he saw a vision of Eden in the fertile shores and admiring people. Settling there would be his aim in 1587. The descriptions in Hariot's text are so detailed, the paintings of John White are so extraordinary, the mind moves to imagine the scene.

————

THE VILLAGE OF CHESEPIUK. John White reaches for his new brushes, made of fine belly hairs of the river otter, wrapped and given to him by the wife of the Chesepiuk chief. His eyes close in gratitude for the kindness of these people and for the visions he has seen in villages from here to Roanoke. Natives dancing around the fire, the coastline green and lush for miles, the water teeming with fishes. There are the strange animals Hariot brings him to draw. At Secotan, a village put together out of grass and poles like a tiny toy city. The charnel houses of bones, where ancestors are laid out to dry like shoe leather. All these things amaze him.

With a prayer that this will not end, he begins another day of work in this extraordinary place. He has made a ground of gray wash on parchment, outlined this woman's figure, with her baby, in black-lead. Now he tints her figure with washes of brown, red, and blue. Later he will highlight her nude form in white and gold. His portfolio lies at his feet—it fascinates these people, and he has had to keep it close by to keep it from disappearing. A few women and children gather as he draws; they laugh and point at the model, who could keep still for hours but for the baby on her back. White squeezes the excess water from his brush with his fingers and feasts his eyes on the moving, living human form displayed before him, limbs and torso exposed to reveal God's architecture.

The hunters have brought back fat venison and twenty sturgeon speared on a pole. Tonight the village will feast. Hariot will show the chief the things he has collected, will offer a fair amount in glass beads, and will ask questions through hand gestures and a few simple words. Hariot is a favorite with the children. He brought small cloth dolls with him to give away. He keeps them in his pocket and they delight in sneaking up and worming their fingers into the hiding place until he catches them and grabs them. They scream and laugh.

Hariot also keeps a list of words that have become useful in conversations with the chief: Wassador, uppowoc, werowance, tapisco. Copper, tobacco, chief, gold. His list is getting longer.

White watches his colleague across the evening fire. Hariot's face glows in the yellow light, his beard glistens with grease from the stew he has been devouring. Every night as Hariot recounts his new finds his face fills with the same excitement White feels when he begins a new drawing. Hariot says the village high priest keeps track of stars and planets—he remembers that same dark sun Hariot noted on their forward voyage. Perhaps it is an omen for them all. Hariot says he has converted some of his Native helpers. At least they seem to listen when he talks about his God.

This has been a fortunate voyage for the both White and Hariot. They are glad to be scouting on their own, away from Lane's soldiers, who tend to fight over small things, so greedy are they for gold. White and Hariot have found no gold, but what they have found is a richness that defies counting. It begins to occur to John White that he could live here for the rest of his life. That this place may be his destiny.

—————

RALPH LANE PROVED LESS THAN SUBTLE in his relations with the Indians. It seems everywhere he went he or his soldiers did harm. To avenge a missing silver cup, one of the men set a whole village on fire. To wrest information about Indian conspiracy, rumored gold mines, and pearls, Lane handcuffed a chief and kidnapped his son. Lane was a long way from following strict instructions that had been given him "[t]hat non shall stryke or mysuse any Indian."[9] The local tribes, at first won over by the "nice clothes" and powerful weapons of the English, grew to resent their violence. Wingina, chief of the Roanoke, had taken the English in; now he plotted with other villages to destroy them. Lane, in turn, plotted a surprise attack on the village and its chief. His men shot Wingina, chased him down, and cut off his head. After that, many coastal tribes became England's mortal enemies. Only Manteo, a Croatoan, would remain a loyal friend.

Lane valued finding gold and pearls over making friends in the wilderness, and he counted on resupply from home. He and his men had built a fort for protection, but a ship they had sent back to England for supplies was late returning and his crew ran short of ammunition and food. Considering the number of Indian enemies they had made, Lane and his men were much relieved when Sir Francis Drake stopped by, ships loaded with booty from a raid of a Spanish settlement down the coast. Drake offered Lane what supplies he could, including food, arms, an extra ship for exploring the sounds. Lane accepted the offer and began loading out supplies. But before they were done a great hurricane blew up, killing some of the crew and scattering and destroying many boats— including the ship meant for Lane.

Lane made a hurried decision to evacuate his men with Drake and come back when they had proper equipment and supplies. To make room for them, Drake's men pitched Lane's books, papers, and pearls into the sea. What popular histories leave out—and Roanoke master historian D.

B. Quinn documents—is that Drake may have also pitched 400 Indian and African slaves into the sea in the midst of the raging storm.

Lane abandoned three of his own men in his haste to leave—the first lost colonists of Roanoke. There is no record of what became of these three, but if they did not starve or die at the hands of their enemies, they may have settled into village life and fathered some blue-eyed Indians.

When Richard Grenville showed up with a supply ship two weeks later, there was no sign of Lane or his men. Grenville left fifteen crewmen to hold the fort. These fifteen would be the second lost colonists. Croatoans would later report that enemy Indians attacked those men, killing several, but that some of them retreated to a small island. No English ever saw them again. A year later, the families of the third venture would come upon the bones of an Englishman.

———

Roanoke Island. June 13, 1586. The wind is rising; cedars and live oaks bend before it, scattering leaves and branches to the forest floor. The water has churned into a froth, bubbling like witches' brew and streaming up the shoreline into the trees. Hailstones the size of hen's eggs pound the dunes. There is no escape from such a storm except by going far inland or out to sea. In their haste Lane's men scramble for the ship, caring little for the trunks full of weaponry and clothing, maps and tools that must be flung overboard to make room. Drake's men haul their human trove from below decks and cast it into the water. For an instant, the captives smell freedom; then the waters scream and groan with the sounds of drowning brown and black men and women; the very air shudders and moans and mutters. The ship heaves to, grinds over the bar and out into open ocean and is gone.

In four days' time, the island will lie silent, battered, and still. A blizzard of seaweed and greenery will cover the sand—greenery tangled with ripe grapes, white pearls, fish, oyster shells, and the bodies of men and women. Some of the bodies will rise, cry out, and stagger into the forest, shadows flashing ebony and chestnut and copper. They will find a way to live, and they are lost.

———

Swansboro, NC. June 1999. I have repaired to a tidy cottage in Swansboro, to read more closely John White's month-by-month log of the 1587 voyage, the one that brought his family to these shores. I flip to the list of names of the colonists, looking for clues to the lives of these extraordinary people.

The ships' roster lists colonists in categories: "Assistants" and men, plus "Women" (seventeen) "Boyes and Children" (nine), "Children born in Virginia" (two, including Virginia), and "Savages" (two, including Manteo, who apparently traveled back and forth between Roanoke Island and England at every turn). Quinn's handy footnotes point out that many of the surnames match up across categories, and there seem to be fourteen family groups. One group includes Ananias Dare, married to Eleanor, who is five months pregnant. Eleanor is the link in what may be the most complex family unit on the voyage: a wife, a husband, a child on the way, and Eleanor's father, soon to be a grandfather—John White, the governor of the colony. Another possible family member is Cutbert White, listed among the men.

What was it like for them to set eyes on these shores for the first time? I dig into the White account, a fascinating tale of life at sea, worry and strife, dissention and trickery. White and the pilot Fernandez do not get along. I sink into an upholstered chair and read for hours. When I raise my head, it's early evening.

I HEAD TO THE WATERFRONT, just a block downhill, find a bench to sit on, stare at the view. English ships sailed up this coast 400 years ago. On July 25, 1587, a boatful of women and children made landfall at Hatteras Island. Is there anybody out there who knows what happened to them? I watch the glittering saltwater, wondering what stories it might tell—and what might lie underneath. Before Swansboro was settled, there was an Algonquin village here. I wonder what they made of those white-sailed ships. I wonder how those people canoed these sounds. I've tried it—a little breeze and you can end up in Cuba. I gaze about, trying to see the water and land from the eyes of an Englishwoman who's just laid eyes on the New World.

My reverie is broken by a bustle of activity at a new restaurant gleaming next to the water. People dressed in summer finery begin to arrive for a sunset dinner. A man in ragged clothes approaches from my left. I watch him from the corner of my eye. He is not dressed for dinner. I am reminded of the homeless people who used to haunt my neighborhood back in Washington, D.C., some of whom I knew well enough to call by name. The ragged man edges toward me slowly, as if a sudden move might scare me away. It occurs to me that I'm sitting on his bench. I turn and say hello.

The ragged man sits down beside me. Over the course of the next few days, Willie will be my "primary source." I'll ask him a lot of questions about Virginia Dare. He will be more interested in pirates. In the course of our conversations, he will confide his life to me: he lives in the back of the fish shack at the end of the block. His children stole his house—he points out a fine colonial on the hill. I don't know whether the stories he tells are based in fact or madness. On my last day in Swansboro, he will pull out a crumpled coupon, a treasured possession, from his pocket and give it to me. It is an entry form for a contest at the local grocery store. The winner gets a party for 50 people, complete with barbecue and all the fixins. I try not to show how moved I am. "If I win," I say, "I'll let you know."

I will carry that coupon around with all my notes and documents for the next year. It seems an important finding of some kind, one too valuable to let go by mailing in for redemption.

But on our first visit, I ask Willie the question I will be asking over and over for the next year: Do you know what happened to Virginia Dare?

"Nope," he says. "But there's pirate treasure buried out there somewhere…" He points across the water.

I trudge back up the hill to find my answers in books.

———

SHARPLY DIVERGING FROM HIS MILITARY STRATEGY, Raleigh's third venture into the New World was led by a civilian and a family man. Why would Raleigh pick an artist to command such a harrowing venture? John White's drawings and maps made up an impressive documentation of the New World. His travel to Chesepiuk had scouted a site for a settlement. Perhaps he had a strong friendship with Manteo, a powerful Indian ally. Perhaps he had personal reasons to want to start a new life; perhaps he had money to invest. In the end, his passion for the New World was his ticket.

His ships' roster listed families and skilled tradesmen rather than soldiers. The purpose of the voyage was to seal, for once and for all, Raleigh's rights in the New World, by populating the land with English children. White brought his pregnant daughter to help guarantee his success.

The presence of women and children is the recurring theme in White's record of command in the same way that treasure was the theme of Ralph Lane's 1585 journals. What was Lane looking for when he came? Gold and pearls. What did he find? No gold, some pearls. What did he leave behind, pitched into the sea in his frantic haste to go home? Pearls, no gold—except for what the Englishmen might have brought when they came.

What was White looking for in 1587? Land and a new life at Chesapeake. Who did he bring with him to make it so? His daughter, at least one other pregnant woman, and several families. What did he leave behind? His daughter and granddaughter, never to be seen again.

———

VIRGIN ISLANDS. JUNE 1587. After two months at sea, White's ships arrive at the isle of Santa Cruz, and the colonists go ashore. White reports, "some of our women . . . by eating a small fruite, like greene apples, were fearfully troubled with a sudden burning in their mouths. . . . Also a child by sucking one of those womens breastes, had at that instant his mouth set on such a burning."[10]

The pilot for the voyage, a Portuguese named Simon Fernandez, is considered one of the best of his time—indeed, he had piloted voyages to these shores with Amadas and Grenville. Yet, heading up the coast, White repeatedly grumbles in his log about Fernandez' judgment and trustworthiness, accusing him of deceptions and miscalculations that bring the ships near ruin. Judging by the tone of White's log entries, one might surmise that he is anxious about the trip, perhaps even worried sick about his colonists, his pregnant daughter. It may be dawning on him that he is in way over his head.

White has no intention of colonizing Roanoke Island, he means only to stop and check on Grenville's men. But when his ships finally arrive there, the maddening Fernandez refuses to take the women and children further up to Chesapeake. Fernandez has plans for privateering, the bread-and-butter of all English ships at sea, and knows the hurricane season may hamper those plans. Perhaps his crew is near revolt, after nearly four months in the company of inaccessible young women. Perhaps he has developed a personal hatred for White after months of mistrust and discord. Whatever the reason, all the families in White's charge are stuck on an island that was never considered a good spot for a colony. Roanoke isn't the land the colonists were promised. The only thing in its favor is its location behind the banks, concealed from passing Spanish eyes.

JULY 25, 1587. Eleanor finally sees what Ananias has been telling her: the huts Lane built are still standing, but they are overgrown with vines, tendrils curling in the open doorways. For an instant she allows herself to think of the cool, misted gardens of home, the boxwood paths, the raked gravel, the order. Roses should climb these walls, she thinks. Then she puts such thoughts away and strides beside her husband, bent on claiming a family home from one of these rude huts. A rustling sound, she turns her head. Deer stand, completely unafraid, in a doorway. It's as if this were their house, Eleanor thinks, alarmed at first, and then amused. She sees the vines are thick with round ripe fruit, some kind of melon. She sees that deer hooves have broken them open, and the rinds have been eaten away. This is what deer eat in the New World, she muses. The baby kicks her, hard. What a marvelous place, she thinks, so abundant, like Eden.

Later, Ananias will find the bones of an Englishman propped up against a wall. The roasted meat of deer that night will be strangely sweet, as if basted in the juice of golden apples.

FINDING THEMSELVES MAROONED AT ROANOKE, the colonists set about cleaning up the huts and building new ones. White, meanwhile, works on renewing good relations with the Croatoan, who will be a critical source of food and protection. He finds them wary, but willing to be friendly under certain terms. They are also close to starving, protective of their meager stores of corn. They show him one of their men who was wounded by Lane and lives crippled with pain. It will be a piece of work to win back the trust of these people.

Within days of arrival, colonist George Howe—perhaps imagining he has found a fisherman's paradise—blissfully wanders off to an estuary to hunt for crabs. He is shot with sixteen arrows, head crushed by many blows, done in by Wanchese and his rebel warriors from the mainland. A friend to the English in the past, now Wanchese is an enemy. The grotesquely excessive attack may reflect continued Native belief that the English have godlike powers—that it would take a great deal to kill one of them.

George Howe leaves behind a fatherless son to make his way in the wilderness. His slaughter is another sign to the colonists that they are sadly mistaken in their faith that this land is Eden, and the Indians will help them.

White finally decides a counterattack is necessary. His men mistakenly go after Manteo's people in a midnight raid on the mainland. White laments "if that one of them, which was a Weroans wife, had not had her childe at her backe, she had been slaine in steede of a man."[11] Only Manteo's diplomacy wins his people back to the English side. It becomes clear that the colonists' only ally in the confederacy of Indian coastal nations is his tiny tribe of Croatoans, who populate a southward island called Hattorask.

On August 13, Manteo is christened and named "Lord of Roanoak," a privilege conferred by Sir Walter Raleigh. On August 18 White logs the birth of a baby girl to "Elenora, daughter to the Governor." The record is brief, but he seems a duly proud grandfather, naming the infant Virginia, in honor of the Virgin Queen and the land the colonists claim. When Virginia is nine days old, White ships out for England, leaving his daughter and granddaughter behind. He has been under constant pressure from the colonists to return for help.

It is the women who finally persuade him to go. Perhaps his own tearful daughter is among them. Perhaps the colonists see all too clearly that they can not last long at Roanoke. Things must have seemed much simpler when White was working under Lane, drawing pictures and smoking pipes of tobacco with the friendly Chesepiuk. Women and children complicate things for John White in the New World.

R<small>OANOKE</small> I<small>SLAND</small>. A<small>UGUST</small> 17, 1587. Eleanor can't forget a story she overheard as a child, that her mother died bearing her, internal organs ripped apart in delivery. She has seen pictures of a lady's internal workings in one of her father's books. With every breath she fights the certainty that her stomach, spleen, womb, liver—all will explode and pour out of her. "Wisakon?" the heathen midwife says. Eleanor sees a dark hand reach out and trickle water from a rag near the corner of her mouth. Manteo's daughter has been nothing but kind, but in Eleanor's fever this face seems to watch her too closely. She turns her head, screams, breathes, clenches her fists.

After a time, it seems the locusts are whining under her skin, her womb is full of locusts, the pain is all over her body. When she opens her eyes, those dark eyes match hers in pain, deep wells of it. Eleanor stares at those sympathetic eyes, nods for a trickle of something cool in her mouth. She sees the rag dangling next to her face, opens her mouth, and sucks.

A<small>UGUST</small> 18. 5:30 A.M. The hour is utterly pink and soft and silent except for the hiss of the tide against the banks of the island and the glassy cries of seabirds. The color blooms, it blooms like a kiss; it blooms like one of these strange curved shells with the rainbow sheen. It blooms across the sky like the rush of fragrant air from the ripening muscadine, it blooms and opens, like the mouth of a baby, sucking for breath and then crying its pure, unbaptized, heathen life.

A<small>UGUST</small> 24. What no one says and everyone knows is this: A babe must be baptized soon in England—sooner still here in the wilds. Most of them will die before gaining a year, some within a week, and the English can't bear to send their infants anywhere but Heaven. John White reads on from his Book of Common Prayer: *"Which of thy great mercy didst save Noe and his family in the ark from perishing by water, and also didst safely lead the children of Israel thy people through the Red Sea . . ."[12]*

"Virginia," John White names her. He forces a smile, terrified to see how tiny she is, how like his own son Thomas when he was brought into this world. Thomas, who did not live to see this day. How can something so small survive

this place? He brushes away a dozen infernal mosquitoes. He drapes the swaddling cloth more closely over the unprotected face. "Five hundred acres for a breeze!" he mutters. He would trade away all that Raleigh has given him for a moment's peace from the whine of these biting insects. Nay, he would allow that whine to accompany him the rest of his life for the assurance that his first grandchild will live.

———

JOHN WHITE'S ATTEMPTS TO MAKE PEACE with the tribes of the mainland are doomed. His best friends will be Manteo's people, who have no food. Grenville's men, long gone, can give no aid. In dire straits, he allows himself to be convinced that hope lies in England.

White ships out on August 27. While weighing anchor, twelve crew members are thrown from the capstan and badly injured. Within a month the undermanned ship suffers a six-day nor'easter of such fury that it will take them thirteen days to get back on course. White glumly reports, "[T]herefore now we expected nothing but by famyne to perish at sea."[13] In October the ship makes the coast of Ireland, but with many crewmembers sick or dead. In Hampton, more than a month later, White learns that Fernandez has returned also—without any prizes. Fernandez' crew, he learns, is so weakened by sickness and diminished by death that they have no strength to bring their boat into the harbor.

Chapter 3:

The Road to Manteo

*America, as everyone knows, is large enough to lose a
child in.*
    —Charles Baxter, *The Feast of Love*

Nothing is secret, that shall not be made manifest.
    —Luke 8:17

PITTSBORO, *N.C. AUGUST 1999.* I am headed to ground zero for the Lost
Colonists: Roanoke Island. From where I live, it's a straight shot east on
Route 64. In 1971, after high school graduation, my best friend and I
took this road on an epic journey all the way from the Great Smoky
Mountains to Hatteras Island. North Carolina was pretty exotic for a
couple of kids from the Maryland suburbs. We ate grits for the first time,
listened to the whine of Tammy Wynette on the car radio, and eyed the
people we met in diners and gas stations warily, wondering if they were
the Klan. I remember how kind people were to two high school girls out
on a lark; we required rescue on a regular basis.

In 1984 I took this same road on a sweep of North Carolina, thinking
I might move here. I remember driving down Hatteras in the April rain,
windows open, slowing to listen to the frogs singing in the ditches. *They
sound like bells, like Tibetan monks, like chanting water.* A nice lady rented
me a whole house for the night, for cheap, and said it was okay for my
dog to sleep on the screen porch. It was pouring. I lay on a bench next to
my dog all night, listening to the rain.

I now live just about halfway between the mountains and the sea, a few miles from Route 64. I don't travel as far east as Roanoke very often.

———

ROUTE 64 EAST. The road has changed some over the years, but toward the coast the land seems much the same. In Everetts, outside Tarboro, the anonymous new four-lane chokes back to a two-lane of particulars: here are tobacco warehouses for sale or lease; tar patches on the road; new vinyl-sided houses next to a field of tobacco stalks with a few crusty yellow leaves still clinging to the tops. One front yard boasts twin cement Venuses, both bashful and turned away. Between Everetts and Williamston the landscape opens up to a wide sky. I see a bank of clouds fat and white as a schooner under full sail—perhaps one of the ghost ships people report along the coast, come to rescue the colonists. Only ninety-seven flat miles to Hatteras.

At the turn for the Outer Banks there is a massive abandoned strip mall, storefronts shored up and their backs caved in, like a ghost town in a Western movie. Cotton fields stretch to either side. Old fields full of broom sedge, white asters, mullein, bindweed. The very land here—tamed and cultivated and long ago wrested from wilderness—seems lost and abandoned. It has been droughty this year. People have left whole corn crops in the field. Just outside of Plymouth, I spy a two-story yellow frame house with front porch columns, entirely wrapped in kudzu. Green tendrils curl over the windowsills and into the empty bedrooms on the second floor.

For some reason, it strikes me profoundly at this moment that for a Yankee, Southern history is the Other. It is what is alien around us that we notice; perhaps that is a survival instinct bred through the ages into the human race—some sixth sense that warns of tigers and other dangers. I have a fascination with the old ways of the South, but I do not pretend to understand them. Understanding seems closest when I can see and touch the artifacts of the perplexing, fearful past: old houses, slave cabins, Confederate statues, farm tools. For years, there have been three antique stores in my town, now there are more like ten. What happened? Maybe our culture has become tired of abandoning its artifacts of history in favor of bland pop culture. Maybe the days of slavery and mass poverty and Reconstruction in the South are so far past now that no one remains who can tell the story—or feel the crushing weight of it. Maybe the layering of legends and interpretations has completely covered up the facts, like kudzu on an abandoned farmhouse.

Maybe some prefer it that way.

One of my vices is watching *Antiques Roadshow*, where people hit it rich with a Tiffany or sag with humiliation at finding their family jewels are fakes. Along with yearning for fortune, however, most people seem to want a good tale, something that might tell them how their great-grandparents must have lived—or anybody in the past. *What is it?* people ask. *What secrets does it hold?* This is the part of the show that gets me on the edge of my seat—this is the treasure I covet. Things that contain time, contain stories.

PITTSBORO, N.C. MAY 1995. Breakfast after the big pig-pickin' for my parents' 52nd anniversary. Scores of Yankees and New Virginians have invaded North Carolina for this event. My uncle Dave waves me over, opens a picture album. A photo of a lean, bearded Confederate soldier peers out of history at me. "Thomas Dixon Falls," my uncle says. "The last surviving color bearer in Pickett's Charge. You're related." You could have knocked me over. My grandmother didn't like to talk about it, he says.

I have since attempted to track down the family "Civil War letters." My mother remembers reading them. Somewhere, in a move, or a death, they were lost or thrown away.

HIGHWAY 64. The road narrows; maritime forests crowd the ditches. A sign reads "Watch for Bears." Another reads "Red Wolf Crossing." I always look for bears and wolves along this stretch. I've never seen one, but I haven't given up hope. The sensation of driving on a smooth paved road through a pine plantation is like gliding into a 3D movie. The rows of trees, passing in formation, doppelgangered into the distance, give a sense of your own motion, as in a dream of flying.

What grows here:

Willow oak, sweet gum, wax myrtle, pine.

The Warren Bridge:

Gliding low over Albemarle Sound.
I open all the windows and pretend I'm on a sailing vessel.
The wind blows my hair from behind, into my mouth, face, eyes.

Landfall, Roanoke Island:

Thirteen yellow sulfur butterflies buffet the breeze to cross the
road.
Where in the world are they going?

MANTEO, N.C. FORT RALEIGH NATIONAL HISTORICAL SITE. I have taken refuge in the air-conditioned visitor center bookstore, perusing stacks of paperbacks on the subject of the Lost Colony. Since April 1941 the park has preserved, studied, and interpreted the colony's history and artifacts. It also hosts the annual outdoor production of Paul Green's symphonic drama, *The Lost Colony*, a draw for tourists by the busload. Between customers, the staff is willing to talk. I ask my litany of questions: Know of anybody descended from the colonists? Have you ever heard a legend about a white doe?

I am in luck. Velton Austin, an off-duty interpretive ranger, has just stopped by for a visit. "I never heard of anyone local who claimed descent from Virginia Dare," he says. If anybody knows local lore, an Austin will. "Austin" is an old family name on Hatteras; Velton is probably related to half the islanders himself. His nickname is R.K., which stands for "Road Kill"—and yes, that's because he's one of those people who salvages road-killed animals and eats or skins them. Turns out he uses skins to make authentic costumes for Native Americans in the play. Earning his nickname, he's gotten a pretty good survey of wildlife over the years, and he's never seen or heard of any white deer in these parts.

"The funny thing is," Austin is saying, "it's the tourists who always claim descent from Virginia Dare." I gather proof is lacking. No one knows anything for sure about Virginia Dare's line of descent, if indeed there was one. What we have instead are family stories and legends, including the one in which she confounds genealogists by turning into a white doe.

The genealogy bug tends to infect people over forty; a hobby that used to involve pilgrimages to county courthouses now has worn pathways on the Internet, which boasts more than 2,000 sites that will find your ancestors. Just as people who claim previous lives tend to claim to have been rich and famous, people tend to want to link their ancestry with kings and queens, generals and courtesans, local heroes and villains. It does not surprise me that people want a connection to Virginia Dare or that it's the people from as far away as California who want to claim something here. Lacking a past that is coherent and place-centered, the American mind leaps to find meaning in a word, a surname, any connection to the mystery.

———

IT'S GETTING TO BE ONE OF THOSE AUGUST AFTERNOONS where the day's buildup of heat merges with a brief rain to create steam. My glasses are fogging, and I'm sweating just walking around. Virginia Dare was born this week, 412 years ago, on this end of the island. I wonder, with my Skin-So-Soft and my tee shirt and tropic weight pants, how in the world her mother managed to make it through an August day in this place. It's not just the heat, it's the mosquitoes.

A few latch on, more hover, zeroing in on my exposed flesh while I hunker down for some calls on the outdoor public phone. You can buy foil pack wipes of bug repellent at the box office here along with programs. The story goes that one fellow, neglecting all warnings to cover up, got up and yelled during the second act: "I know where those damn people went. The mosquitoes up and carried them away!" Archeological surveys show that Indian villages always clustered on the northerly shores of inlets on the Albemarle and Pamlico sounds. Not only did they provide protection from nor'easters in winter, prevailing breezes kept the skeeters away in summer.

The path from the visitor center to the Waterside Theater is quiet. I have only the whine of mosquitoes to keep me company. In the afternoon light, the theater is stunning. I had not known the backdrop for the set was Albemarle Sound. Here the birth of Virginia Dare is played out night after night in the summer months. I check the light: The sun will set just as the play begins; the moon will rise, full, just over there.

———

A FEW YEARS BACK, I worked in a university building in Chapel Hill, across the street from a cemetery. I wrote poetry on my lunch hour there, sometimes sitting in the gazebo, sometimes on the old rock wall. One day I discovered, on a well-worn path, the grave of Paul Green, North Carolina's most beloved playwright, teacher and historian, champion of the underdog. His plays and stories broke open the hidden lives of rural African Americans and tenant farmers, giving voices to people who had none. His life became a beacon to progressive politics in the state. A short walk from his grave is an outdoor theater made of rock ledges and set in a forest. Although it's not named for him, I've always thought of this as "Paul Green's theater." I've always imagined plays set here in the thirties and forties, with flaming torches, song and tragedy. I admit it: I used to climb on stage sometimes with a friend from work. She would shout out poems in Russian and I would shout out mine in English, to imaginary crowds.

I still go in pilgrimage to Green's grave sometimes, leave small tributes: acorns, oak leaves, blades of grass. His gravestone reads: PAUL GREEN / TEACHER, DRAMATIST, PHILOSOPHER. Under his wife's name: LOVE IS THE SOUL OF MAN.

Until I went to Manteo, I had never seen one of his plays.

———

8 P.M. WATERSIDE THEATER, MANTEO. Watching the tourists fill the darkening bowl of the amphitheater, I can hear friends calling to friends, moms negotiating peace among siblings, the murmur of anticipation and satisfaction you hear in summer crowds. I realize, suddenly, that I am probably the only person here by myself. Outdoor theater is a social ritual—especially for families with children. I push a familiar feeling firmly away. I am here to work. I am here to take notes. But as the light dims, memory rises.

In 1993, at age thirty-nine, long after I had given up hope for it, I found myself pregnant. The little pink cross on the test strip surprised me so much I almost fell down the stairs, calling to my husband. For years I had imagined a child playing in the orchard of my farm, a two-year-old scrambling in the clover, an eight-year-old climbing trees. At a children's Christmas pageant one year I made one of those deals with God that six-year-olds make: *If only you will let me have this thing, I promise to be good.* When it happened, I felt as personally blessed as Mary, or perhaps her barren kinswoman Elizabeth.

Four months in, I finally relaxed and told the news to my friends and to my stepdaughter. Her eyes got big at the prospect of a new brother or sister. I was still very unsure that this was real. Finally, my breasts swollen and my diet confined to crackers, I began to allow myself to succumb to the craving for the milk smell of a baby's head, the tender weight against my belly, the spill of life in my hands. I had my second doctor visit; I heard that heartbeat, fine and strong as a freight train coming. The next day we went for a sonogram. There she was: tiny fingers and toes, pudgy face, floating. *Look, look,* I kept saying. *There she is.*

That moment has congealed in my mind, water becoming ice. At that exact moment, they told me she was dead.

Obsessed with that image, for years afterward I refused to speak of her. I spent hours writing endless poems that listed everything I ever knew that died. Finally, I named her: Emily for the poet; Day for my husband's mother's family, and for the light of day she never saw. I buried her ashes and left no marker. At the burial, two small children were playing in the graveyard. They solemnly asked if they could watch. I said yes. What else could I say? They had just buried their mother.

I have never had the heart to try again. I have put it out of my mind. Sometimes though I look around me, at the beach or in a shopping mall, any place where there are large gatherings of people, and get a jarring sense of being unhooked from the life of the world, from my own life, like a train car uncoupling from the string—disconnected, watching, over to one side.

————

LIKE THE *BOOK OF COMMON PRAYER*, the Constitution of the Iroquois Nation contains rituals for infant funerals:

Then shall you gather the little boys and girls at the house of mourning and at the funeral feast a speaker shall address the children and bid them be happy once more, though by a death, gloom has been cast over them. Then shall the black clouds roll away and the sky shall show blue once more. Then shall the children be again in sunshine.[1]

One by one as they learned of my loss, women came to me and told me of their own lost children or dreams of children. I have learned that there is a secret nation of women who have miscarried or lost children or both—and never speak of it except in hushed tones, to others of that clan.

———

THE PLAY IS A SPECTACLE. Next to me sits a young couple with a ten-year-old boy.

"Have you seen this before?" I ask the dad.

"When I was a kid," he says.

"Was it good?" I ask.

"All I remember," he grins, "is a lot of Indian dancing and a big noise."

The scenes pass in a colorful display: Queen Elizabeth and the ladies of the court in their glittering dresses; Raleigh in *his* glittering dress; an amusing sidekick who drinks too much; the commoners having a picnic. Paul Green has picked Eleanor Dare for his heroine, and she does a good job of it. She is the center of a romantic triangle; she makes persuasive arguments for letting women go to the New World, actually facing off with the queen of England in one scene. She acts as a community leader amidst strife and starvation: The myth of the strong woman.

There's a great sword fight with evil Fernando, the Spanish pilot. There's an Indian dance with nods to John White's famous drawings. There's a "big noise" when Ralph Lane shoots Wingina (sorry, kids, no beheadings). Virginia is born and baptized, played by a bundle of swaddling clothes just like Jesus in a Christmas play; unlike Jesus, however, she does not remain the center of attention. It's her mother, Eleanor, who takes control of the stage.

Lacking much in the way of documentation for the colonists' movements after they came ashore, Paul Green was faced with making things up. What he picked were possibilities that were dramatically pleasing, not necessarily accurate. Green wrote a story for his time—1937, when the Great Depression and a looming war in Europe had left Americans hungry and despondent and fighting amongst themselves. His play struck a great chord when it first came out, perhaps because Eleanor's courage points to a great national myth: Americans have always pulled together when the chips are down.

————

THE PLAY ENDS WITH ELEANOR leading the frightened colonists into the wilderness toward an unknown future, toting bag and baggage and sleeping children. It's affecting. The great impression of this scene, however, comes after we all begin to head back to our cars:

> *A footlit walkway meanders through the dark, live oaks hung with Spanish moss.*
> *The play's final scene reprises: a throng of tired people carrying their great treasures, beautiful sleeping children.*
> *One man hoists a two-year-old onto his shoulders; her head rests on his.*
> *Her hair glows, backlit, in fine whorls and wisps.*
> *The walk is long, the pathway dim, the faces in shadow, dark shapes in the forest. I trudge beside strangers, as if in a dream of common exile.*

————

BODIE ISLAND, SOUND SIDE. AUGUST 1999. I wake early, walk out to the Sound. I planned to put my whole body into Currituck on this trip—a kind of ritual baptism in the waters that the colonists must have crossed in their journey. I imagined it balmy and sea-blue and about three feet deep as I've seen it before here at my aunt's beach house in Duck. But the water is murky and gunmetal gray and cold, the chop slapping hard at the retaining wall. I recall a day like this a year ago, when the rising wind was so strong it smacked two-foot waves on the faces of cousins rescuing a small boat in a post-hurricane gale.

Strong winds from far away always give notice of their arrival on the

Outer Banks. There's a hurricane brewing today, heading this way. Chickenhearted, I stay the heck out of the water.

Historians say that the colony most likely split up. Some probably moved north, up Currituck, to seek the Chesepiuk Indian village that was their original destination. Some would have gone south, down Hatteras—also called Croatoan—to keep watch with Manteo and his people for John White's return. Either way, they crossed some part of this enormous water.

On the radio this morning, between reports of the erratic approach of Hurricane Dennis, I hear news of a gigantic sea turtle the size of a VW bug sighted in the waters under New York's Verrazzano Bridge. "We didn't know what it was," a ship's captain says. The Coast Guard frees it from a trotline and it paddles away, hugely and mysteriously, into the tide.

In 1524 Verrazzano explored the waters from Cape Fear, N.C., to Nova Scotia. Perhaps such tortoises were a common sight in his time. In June 1587, near what is now St. Croix, John White and his men caught "5 great tortoises"—one so large that it took sixteen men to carry it. In the early days of the Americas, such wonders abounded. The land and waters bulged with extraordinary riches. Like Eden, only scary.

Manteo, Sir Walter Raleigh Street. Historian lebame houston[2] gives fair warning: I may catch the mother of all colds if I stay in the same room with her for any length of time. "We've all got it," she says, with a grimace to her research assistant Barbara Hird, who coughs discretely in agreement. Then houston lights a cigarette and proceeds to tell everything she knows about Virginia Dare and the Lost Colony and all the folks out there making up stories about them. "The worst one I can remember, is that *novelist*. He has them all walk *overland* to Florida. Imagine."

"It's all swamps," I protest.

"Exactly," says houston.

What would make imagination take such unlikely turns? I will later scan this novel at UNC-Chapel Hill's North Carolina Collection. It ends with our hero burying his account of the tale in a copper box under the sand, like gold doubloons and pieces of eight, hoping to preserve it for all time. I love how he equates stories with treasure; I love that he co-opts Florida and all its DeSotoesque mystique, absorbing it, amoebalike, into the Roanoke tale.

Houston has just finished the theater season with her two plays, *Bloody Mary and the Virgin Queen*, and *Elizabeth R.*, in which Hird, an English actress, takes starring roles. Hird played Elizabeth in *The Lost Colony* for ten years. Houston has researched and written many pages of educational materials for the park in years past. I've got a few of them in my car. Now a new project consumes her: Identifying a gold signet ring found at Buxton, N.C., in the crook of the elbow of Hatteras Island. Archeologist David Phelps, a noted North Carolina scholar of Native American culture, discovered the ring at the site of an Indian village that may very well be "Croatoan," where Manteo's people lived. The ring is sixteenth century, houston says, possibly from one of the men of the Lost Colony. She and Hird are scanning the colonists' family crests and genealogies to trace it.

Identifying who the colonists were, houston explains, is key to figuring out why they came, how they might have handled adversity, and even where they went. That makes sense to me. You've got to know your characters if you're going to make up a story. If the colonists were helpless, effete, upper-crust types, for example, they might not have had the skills to adapt to the grueling circumstances in which they found themselves. They might not have gotten far. If they were yeomen carpenters and farmers and stone masons and boat builders, they may have had a better chance, wherever they went.

By researching the ring's heraldic crest, Hird and houston have surmised it belonged to a member of the Kendall family. There were two Kendalls at Roanoke: One is Abraham Kendall, a famous sixteenth-century shipmaster who sailed with Drake. "But that would be too easy," houston laughs. The other is a more obscure Master Kendall who traveled with Ralph Lane's expedition. "You know damn well it's going to be that one," she grumps. "He'll be harder to find." I get the idea she's enjoying the challenge.

Identifying a coat of arms, houston explains, involves finding the first use of the crest from court records and deeds and indentures. Complicating this search is the fact that all such records in London were moved during the Second World War; English archivists are still working on getting things back in order. Houston has gotten as far as checking probate records but has not yet found wills for either Kendall. The normal practice in those days was for a single will to be recorded, in a parish or guild hall—no multiple copies left around hither and yon to make things easy. If a far traveler disappeared, or did not return when expected, after a period of years he would be declared "dead beyond the seas" and his will would take effect. The search continues for a Kendall will.

Meanwhile, houston tells me, she has tracked a number of other colonists back to their English roots. Eleanor Dare, she says, was christened May 7, 1568, at St. Martin's Ludgate, a hundred yards from St. Paul's Cathedral in London. Her mother was Thomasine Cooper White, married to John White in 1566. Thomasine's first child was a son, Thomas, who died the year Eleanor was born. Houston has been able to find a 1580 indenture relating to John White.

The problem with tracking John White, she says, is that he was not a famous painter; he was in the painters and stainers guild but not on any lists for big court projects. In fact, in lebame houston's opinion, White was a mediocre painter at best, whose weak point was the human form. As evidence, she brings out an edition of White's watercolors and turns to Plate 47, a full-length portrait of an Indian woman with two right feet. The error was duly corrected in later engravings by Theodor De Bry, who created printable, popularized versions of White's work.

Another difficulty in tracking John White is that he has a commonplace name: There have been many false leads. Because so many children never made it to adulthood in those days, houston explains, it was common practice to use a name over and over again in a single family. Sometimes a man would name all his sons John, and they would be known as John the elder, John the middle, and so on. "The only name," she says, "I've seen on the ship's roster that has never been repeated is Ananias."

In the fifties, historian William Powell worked to identify some of the colonists by their memberships in guilds. Some historians have concluded from guild membership that the colonists must have been skilled workers, including among them a shoemaker, goldsmith, tailor, basket maker, and farmer. But houston points out that in sixteenth-century London, guild membership was almost required in order to enjoy certain rights. It did not necessarily indicate a person's job or class.

"Ben Jonson, the writer, was a member of the Bricklayers Guild," she says, "and he never laid a brick. Prince Charles is a member of the Fishmongers Guild."

White's twelve assistants were each responsible for recruiting a certain number of colonists. Some of the colonists were related, some shared guild membership. Assistant George Howe, for example, was in the painters guild like White, and he brought his own son George. Another example: although listed separately on the ship's roster, Ambrose Viccars was likely married to Elizabeth Viccars, and the Ambrose Viccars listed under "boys" is surely the junior edition.

It's safe to assume, houston says, that when surnames in the women's roster match those on the list of men (or come close, White was a terrible speller), they indicate wives or sisters. A woman in sixteenth-century England would not have been able to claim the 500 acres per colonist in her own name, but her presence could have padded the acreage of a male relation. Some of the women on the list may have been servants or wet nurses. "Usually in a voyage there was a doctor," houston says. "There's no evidence of that here. Usually there was a chaplain, and there should have been one. If there wasn't, there was a reason." Perhaps the colonists were breaking from the Church of England. Perhaps their prayers and baptisms were those of a new Protestant sect.

What about the identity of Simon Fernandez, the pilot who left the colonists stranded on Roanoke? Was he really a Spanish spy? Did he plot to foil the colony? Houston says—quite matter-of-factly—that Fernandez was no Catholic and no Spaniard. He was Portuguese, a member of the Lutheran Church in London, and was in court for piracy a lot (no doubt preying on Spanish treasure ships). Paul Green's loathsome Spanish villain a Lutheran? The facts defy the myth.

Houston is a kind of unofficial historian for the Lost Colony play and Waterside Theater. Her mother was business manager of the theater for many years and worked with Paul Green when he was staging the play. Houston reports that locals, state leaders, and national groups all jumped into the project with both feet. President Roosevelt helped raise money for it by designing a five-cent Virginia Dare stamp. "By now," houston says, "the show has a life of its own. People bring their kids because it's history, but it's the history of the show that brings them as much as anything else." Green dramatized the history as a love story, houston explains, but also as an inspirational statement: "You can make it through hard times—like John and Eleanor did."

The Indian dancers in the first production were members of the Civilian Conservation Corps, and most of the actors were from Manteo. A choice few were imported from the Federal Theater Project in New York. People were lucky to get work; it was the Depression. Actors received room and board and a small fee, paid in commemorative coins, a dollar a show.

Houston brings out her precious collection of coins, fifty-cent pieces minted by the U.S. Treasury just for this event. "There were 25,000 of these made," she says. "The head of Sir Walter was modeled after Errol Flynn." The coin is beautifully embossed, gleaming, silver. And, yes, it does look like Errol Flynn. On the other side, Eleanor Dare clutches her baby, gazes out at a ship under sail, her skirts swept back in a stiff breeze.

The souvenir program published for the 1937 premiere of *The Lost Colony* contains an interview with the artist who designed the coin, sculptor William Mark Simpson from Baltimore. "I've modeled [Eleanor] standing there courageously," he says, "facing uncertainty with pride and determination, but always with the thought of her native England . . ."[3] I page through for references to Virginia, what she means, who she will be: On the title page, under "350th Anniversary Celebration," the program boasts it celebrates "The Beginning of Anglo-American Civilization," along with the birth of Virginia Dare. Tucked into a later section is an advertising spread, featuring a full-page rendition of Virginia's face, in bonneted and beribboned glory. The ad is selling Virginia Dare wine, made from the scuppernong grape. Not claiming an original Colony recipe, the Garrett winery does tout its product as an "*original* American wine," first bottled in 1835, "near the place where Raleigh's Lost Colony landed..."[4]

As an Englishwoman, Barbara Hird finds it interesting that the Lost Colony, Raleigh's pet project, was never mentioned in history courses where she grew up. "I had to come here to find out about it," she says. Now, more than sixty years after the first production of *The Lost Colony*, three million people have seen the play. For years it has been the public's prime source of information—and misinformation—on the subject of the Roanoke settlement. Until the play came out, houston says, the colony wasn't a big focus in North Carolina history classes, much less in national history. "It's not surprising, though," she says, with a wry grin. "The colony was a failure. You wouldn't want to celebrate that sort of thing."

I remember a call I made to a museum a while back, asking about North Carolina women's history in general and Virginia Dare in particular. "Good *luck*," the woman who answered the phone said in a frustrated tone, as if to say, *There isn't any.*

Apparently scholarly interest in the Lost Colony lapsed for a time until 1955, when historian D. B. Quinn published *The Roanoke Voyages, 1584-1590.* This extraordinary resource book contained in two volumes an astonishing array of original source material on the subject, including letters, royal decrees, ships' logs, spy reports, court records, and explorers' journals. Quinn's collection included translations of Spanish court records that shed much new light on the fate of the colony.

Of course, not everyone gets the history right—even the easy stuff. Houston tells this story: "Queen Elizabeth, the Virgin Queen, right? Never married, never had children. A couple of years back we had this big event for the 400th anniversary. Princess Anne came, and the governor introduced her as a *direct descendent* of Queen Elizabeth."

I'm imagining the look on Princess Anne's face.

And what does houston think happened to Virginia Dare? "The chances of her surviving very long were not very good," she says. "She probably died on Roanoke Island. She was born on the eighteenth, christened on the twenty-fourth, and John White left shortly thereafter. As a rule, in London, people tried to christen their children within the first three days, because often they didn't make it much beyond that."

And what of the rest of the colonists?

"I think—based on no evidence, mind you—that the bulk of the colony did what they intended to do in the first place. They went to Chesapeake, to the land they actually owned. It makes sense to me that a holding party either went back to Croatoan or stayed here to lead Governor White to the new site."

She takes a deep drag from her cigarette, coughs, and crushes the butt. "I'll be damned," she says, "if I would wait out on Roanoke Island for three years for somebody to show up and rescue me."

LONG AFTER I HAVE LEFT LEBAME HOUSTON'S COZY LIVING ROOM—and long since I've recovered from "the mother of all colds"—I will learn that her "Kendall ring" theory is not without controversy. Wynn Dough, former curator of the Outer Banks History Center says, regarding the Kendall ring, "I'm a heretic. I don't know how you can link somebody to a piece of gold with a lion on it." He explains that signet rings were something like the cell phones of the sixteenth century—they were a dime a dozen. Lions, roses, and thistles were common devices on them. On the other hand, he admits, "*If* it belonged to a colonist, [the Buxton site] would be a good place for it to show up. It's a definite maybe." His thinking is that there were plenty of lonely and lecherous English guys around over the years who might have traded gold rings for favors.

Dough was raised on Roanoke Island, so he grew up on the Lost Colony mystery. His great grandfather once owned the land where the colony settled. His theory about where the colonists went? He reminds me that each of the twelve assistants gathered his own group of colonists. "If things started turning to crap, they probably busted up faster than a PTA meeting, each group following its own leader. The only thing that 'CROATAN' signifies is that at least one literate colonist went to Hatteras."

Chapter 4:

In Search of Rosebud

A whole country of English is there, man; bred of those that were left there in '79.
—from *Eastward Hoe*, an Elizabethan
play referencing the Lost Colony

MANTEO. AUGUST 1999. Gale warning is one flag: red square, black in the middle. Hurricane is two. From the blasts of wind and unsettled sky I'm guessing Dennis is finally headed this way. It doesn't look good for chartering a boat, and hiring a pilot from the local airfield to fly me around is equally iffy. So I'm plotting an overland route: up the Outer Banks to Elizabeth City, N.C., then across the Great Dismal Swamp and over the James River to Jamestown Island, in Virginia. At Jamestown I hope to talk to some archeologists who've worked at Roanoke. And, along the way, I'm hoping to get a sense of the landscape the colonists may have traveled on their way to Chesapeake.

First another cup of McDonald's coffee for a last ditch pilgrimage to the Salty Dawg Marina. In the fast food line I chat with a retired man and his wife, tell them about my search. With typical North Carolina kindness, they worry about me traveling alone. They tell me all they know about Virginia Dare, and even invite me to their home, giving directions. I think of Manteo's tidy neighborhoods, carefully tended lawns, gardens blooming with hot pink petunias and oleander. I'm tempted to stay in this safe harbor, but I must move on if I'm going to beat the storm.

At the boatyard flags are snapping; halyards clang. I drive down a sand track to the trailer in back, the marina office. The place seems dim and uninhabited, but the door is open. I call out. Someone answers. I have come at a bad time; nobody busier than a boatyard owner the day before a hurricane. No boats to rent here, and I must be crazy to ask. Besides, from here to the Great Dismal is a long way over water. Before I go, I get a name: Rosebud Fearing. He's the man to talk to in Elizabeth City. He's not hard to find, hangs out downtown by the Intracoastal Waterway. He has stories to tell, and knows people with boats. Might get a good tale or two out of Rosebud.

―――――

ROUTE 158 ZIPS UP HATTERAS, crosses over Currituck Sound, and continues north on a narrow spit of mainland wedged between the sound and the North River. For a time the road parallels the most remote section of the Outer Banks, passing towns named Harbinger, Spot, and Mamie; then Grandy, Bertha, and Coinjock. A road at Coinjock takes a jog east to Waterlilly. Sucker for a pretty name, I am tempted to make the turn. But I keep on. The road just about runs out of places to go, hooks west toward Belcross, then crosses the northern tip of another finger of Albemarle Sound, the Pasquotank River. Finally, Elizabeth City.

Rain dashes against the windshield but I have outrun the hurricane so far. It seems to be wavering indecisively southeast of here. By following signs to the other side of town I find the Museum of the Albemarle, a neat square brick building tucked into the side of the road like a small-town library.

Exhibit designer Don Pendergraft doesn't mind spinning a few tales about the Lost Colony. There's the "Lost Schooner of the Dismal Swamp"—an especially good one for hurricane season. Sometime in the 1930s, a boy reported finding the ribs of a sixteenth-century sailing vessel deep in the heart of the Dismal Swamp, north of here. Local folks became convinced that it belonged to the Lost Colony. As the story goes, the colonists must have spied a monster hurricane coming, loaded up their pinnace, and sailed up Albemarle to the Chowan River. The storm surge was so mighty that it caught their boat, lifted it, and dropped it in the middle of the Great Dismal.

44

"That's a pretty far stretch," Pendergraft says. I think of the map I've been following, all those finger-shaped rivers—small bays, really—gripping the watery landscape. I imagine the pinnace surging upward, then spinning into the air in a passing tornado, like Dorothy's house in *The Wizard of Oz*. It makes a great story. What was found at Roanoke in 1590 may support the idea that a monster hurricane came along at some point. The houses were razed, not burned; a hurricane can do that. No historian ever examined the wreck the boy found, however, and its location has long since been lost. I'm impressed that people living in the Great Dismal remembered the story of the Lost Colony as if it belonged to them, not to the history books. They took the evidence before them and spun a fantastic tale to answer the same question I've been asking: Whatever happened to Virginia Dare?

According to one of John White's maps, the village of Chesepiuk lay at the entrance to the Chesapeake Bay, at a confluence of great estuaries, no doubt rich with bluefish and sturgeon, oysters and crabs. To the west lay the mouths of the James and York Rivers, as yet unnamed. The hump of land between Albemarle Sound and the mouth of the Chesapeake Bay is bland and featureless on White's map, virtually unexplored except for a few waterways dotted with Indian villages.

On a modern map, the broad finger of Currituck peters out into the northern shallows of Back Bay, and Carolina's Outer Banks finally fuse to the mainland in Virginia. Modern cartographers fill in broad sections of land between Albemarle Sound and the Chesapeake with watery dots and dashes indicating swamp. At the heart of the wetlands is a vast green oblong, the Great Dismal. In the past four centuries or so, we have filled in a few blank places on John White's map.

What route did the colonists take if they went north to Chesepiuk? The choice seems simple—go by water. The swampy, unexplored mainland would have seemed impenetrable. On the other hand, any boat trip to the Indian village of Chesepiuk would have required slipping through the treacherous bars of the Outer Banks, sailing boldly into the open Atlantic—taking the chance of exposure to Spanish ships—before scurrying into the protected waters past Cape Henry. A safer route might entail slipping up one of the inlets of Albemarle Sound to its far inland reaches. At some point, the water would have turned to wetland and it was a rugged, soggy hike to the Chesapeake shore.

Were there paths through the Dismal Swamp? Could Indian friends have guided the colonists safely to the Chesepiuk settlement on the other side? But for the modern canal cut through the Dismal, it still looks impenetrable. Pendergraft grew up in these parts, and in his opinion, walking through the swamp would have been impossible. I remind him that English explorer John Lawson and his Indian guides walked all over North and South Carolina, including some pretty swampy places. "But Lawson was a type A personality," he laughs. Lawson had an Indian woman as a guide for a time, but no English women and children. Children complicate travel, as any parent on a great American road trip surely knows: *Are we there yet?*

Pendergraft, part Native American, has heard just one legend about white deer: his uncle used to say that rubbing the gallstone of a white deer on your skin will "take the fire out of you." Deer have gallstones? I'm learning all kinds of new things. There's a small library at the museum, behind the exhibit area. In these books you can find a legend about almost anything to do with the Great Dismal. Longfellow wrote a poem about escaped slaves hiding in the gloom there:

> *Where will-o-wisps and glow worms shine*
> *In bullrush and brake;*
> *Where waving mosses shroud the pine,*
> *And the cedar grows and the poisonous vine,*
> *Is spotted like the snake . . .*[1]

There's a ballad about the ghost of an Indian maid:

> *all night long by firefly lamp,*
> *She paddles her white canoe.*[2]

There are legends about white snakes, witches, runaway slaves, and spirits. And finally, here is a legend about a white doe. It's a complicated story, about a chief's beautiful daughter, an old mother deer, a silver arrow, and a rattlesnake. The Indian girl escapes certain death by transforming into a white doe. I have found my white doe legend—or have I? In this story the doe has a crimson spot on her forehead—and there ain't no English girls with flowy blonde hair in it.

THE STORY GOES ROSEBUD FEARING got his nickname from his habit of welcoming boaters who get this far up the Intracoastal Waterway by presenting them with a red rose. This I'd love to see. I call his house. No answer. I knock on his door. No one home. For the next hour, I will be in search of Rosebud, dogging his tracks. I go to the Colonial Restaurant, where he always has lunch this time of day; no dice (good iced tea, though). I track him to Water Street, where he is known to hang out. The sky has changed back to August steam. It's blazing hot, and all but deserted:

A fellow catching crabs.
An SUV, air conditioning on, facing the water.
A woman inside, eating a sandwich, staring out across the sound.

No Rosebud.

I walk to the end of the waterfront. A couple of young women are setting up a flea market under a shaded awning. There's scads of stuff, including an entire bag full of cat toys. I don't have a cat, but I know somebody who does. It's a dollar. I buy it, just to have something in hand.

IF THE COLONISTS TRAVELED UP ALBEMARLE SOUND or Currituck and made their way overland to Chesepiuk village, I don't see how they did it. Historians say they may have survived somewhere in this region, living in peace among the Natives, for as long as twenty years. Pocahontas's father, chief Powhatan, claimed to have "miserably slaughtered" them all in his bid for power in the Chesapeake region in the early 1600s, but reports kept coming of survivors. After John White gave up the search, other English attempts were made to check on the colonists in later years. Raleigh himself—perhaps thinking to keep hold of his patent, perhaps belatedly struck by guilt—sent a ship to search for them in 1602, but found nothing. Still, reports kept coming—from settlers at the new colony of Jamestown.

In the spring of 1607 this new band of English planters made a colony on an island hugging the north shore of the mile-wide James River. Finally England had a settlement at Chesapeake. This colony was not immune to Indian attack, starvation, and political upheaval; it would be a piece of work to keep the colony alive. But they survived—tantalizingly close to the places where a few Roanoke survivors may have held on. That the heirs to Roanokers' dreams might have saved Roanoke survivors is a tempting speculation.

One Jamestown settler wrote of seeing "a savage boy about the age of ten yeeres, which had a head of haire of perfect yellow and a reasonable white skinne, which is a miracle amongst all savages."[3] Most of the sightings named locations across the James River, near the Chowan. John Smith reported Indian talk of "certain men cloathed at a place called Ocanahonan." ("Men cloathed" was how Indians spoke of the English.) Jamestown secretary William Strachey received reports that at Peccarecamek and Ochanahoen "the people have houses built with stone walls, and one story above another, so taught them by those English who escaped the slaughter at Roanoak." Strachey also reported that in 1610 "at Ritanoe, the weroance Eyanoco preserved seven of the English alive—four men, two boys and one young maid (who escaped and fled up the River Chanoke)." With this report there were maps showing where English lived, and reports of letters and crosses on trees.

Could that maid have been Virginia Dare? Possibly, but if she was alive she was twenty-three—more like an old maid than a young one by English—or Indian—standards. Could it have been her daughter? Perhaps. If Virginia Dare had survived after Powhatan's wars, she most likely did so by joining an Indian family. A daughter may have retained some remnant of English garb—a scrap of bonnet, a pink ribbon. She may have mouthed scraps of the English language, the way second generation American immigrants can swear and pray a few words of their parents' native tongue.

A few Lost Colonists may have survived within fifty miles of Jamestown as captives or slaves in Indian villages. A few others may have survived at the Croatoan village and intermarried. Back at Roanoke in the early 1700s, John Lawson viewed the fort in ruins and reported Indian claims of English ancestry at Hatteras: "These tell us, that several of their Ancestors were white People, and could talk in a Book, as we do; the Truth of which is confirm'd by gray Eyes being found frequently amongst these Indians, and no others."[4] In later years, some Hatteras Indians may have migrated inland as English settlers and tribal wars encroached upon coastal lands. Legend has it that some Lost Colony blood still survives, many generations later, among the Lumbee of Robeson County.

WHAT HAPPENED AFTER THE LOST COLONISTS waved good-bye to John White? They left within months. In the spring of 1588, a small Spanish vessel sailed to Chesapeake to spy on a rumored English colony. Unable to find anything at Chesapeake, the ship headed south, still unaware that the colony had settled at Roanoke Island. As chance would have it, the captain slipped behind the Outer Banks to escape strong winds. Somewhere between where he entered Pamlico Sound and where he exited, the captain encountered "a slipway for small vessels, and on land a number of wells made with English casks, and other debris indicating that a considerable number of people had been there."[5] It could have been nothing other than the abandoned village at Roanoke.

John White knew nothing of this discovery; it was part of secret reports to the king of Spain in February 1600. White began plotting his return to Roanoke as soon as he reached England in the fall of 1587. By the time he arrived in England, however, the queen had already placed a moratorium on shipping, with the intent of gathering a force of ships powerful enough to ward off the Spanish fleet. Still, White did not give up hope. He tirelessly sought backers to help finance the journeys, finding Raleigh and Grenville among his supporters. Always, expenses were high, and it was expected that active piracy would gain financial prizes that would keep investors from bankruptcy. White's plan was not to rescue the colonists but to resupply them and bring yet more planters to fortify the settlement. Finally, in April 1588, White was able to wrest two small vessels for a voyage. Accompanied by a small troop of planters, White sailed into disaster. After capturing some prizes, White's ships were attacked and looted. All the supplies were taken. The captain got a pike stuck through his head. Three planters were wounded. White was wounded in several places, including his hindquarters. He and his planters were lucky to be alive.

Despite this disaster, White and Raleigh were able to gain a new group of backers, but the ships did not sail until March of 1590. At the last minute, the captain refused to allow supplies and planters aboard ship. Only White was taken on board. Again, piracy ruled the voyage. The ships spent months in the West Indies and finally made it to the Outer Banks in August. As the crew approached Roanoke, gale-force winds and raging tides swamped a landing boat, and seven were drowned, including the captain and ship's surgeon.

Finally, on August 18, White made it ashore. There he found the colonists gone, and the houses torn down, but a new fort still standing. His paintings and papers were ruined, and CROATOAN and CRO were carved into posts. "Croatoan" signaled the colonists' new location. "Cro" remains mysterious—was it carved in haste, then abandoned? There was no cross carved above, the mark that would indicate distress. Croatoan was only fifty miles away, but White never made it.

While heading to Croatoan village, ships were caught in another storm that ripped out anchor cables and threatened to drive them into the shore. The ships were lucky to escape being dashed to pieces. Without anchors they could not continue to take risks in the shoal waters of the Outer Banks and sounds. White's ships attempted to head for the West Indies, then the Azores, to winter over, but storms dogged their moves. They went home without getting close to Croatoan. White had lost his the chance to find out if his colonists or his kin were living.

The privateering vessels that were part of the 1590 voyage had some success, but White saw none of the profits and Raleigh saw little. The settlement worked its way through the maritime courts. In February 1593 White sent an account of his last voyage to Richard Hakluyt, who would later publish it. In his letter to Hakluyt, White concluded that this was just one among many cursed voyages, and that he was hereby "committing the reliefe of my discomfortable company the planters in Virginia, to the merciful help of the Almighty."[6]

He had given up on Virginia Dare.

HATTERAS ISLAND. NOVEMBER 1587. Eleanor bundles her baby and her belongings and hoists them aboard the pinnace. The Croatoans—what's left of them after the fever struck three weeks ago—say the bad storm time is over. But there is so little to eat in their village that just a few men stay behind to winter over and eat fish and watch for Father. Others have headed into the mainland in a desperate search for game. The rest are going to the village of Chesepiuk—the only friendly Indian place they know of, any more, besides Croatoan. They will travel in the patched up pinnace and in canoes rigged with sails, for the weather is right just today and will no doubt change soon.

Father told a few men the way to the Indian village. Eleanor carries signs of friendship from those people: a copper plate; a pipe; a deerskin bag of pearls.

Whether they will be welcomed or not after all this time, no one knows. All they know is that they must go. The children are hungry, tired of chewing on parched corn. Hostile tribes on the mainland have kept hunters from going ashore. Ananias was one of the first to try—his body came back quilled with arrows.

Eleanor has seen bucks with enormous racks of horns swimming across Albemarle in search of something green. She has seen does and their spotted fawns rib-sprung, gaunt, chewing seaweed. More than once she has found and buried a fawn whose pelt is peeled back by birds, eye sockets hollow and dry, lips white with salt. Eleanor has never seen such dry land. A whirling ash will set miles of scrub to burning. Some of the Croatoan say the English have put a curse on things. Even the fish wash up on shore, crusted with salt and flies.

They will sail north from Croatoan to Roanoke, scavenge what they can, and head up the shoal waters, sneaking out through Trinity Harbor and chancing it that their many enemies are busy elsewhere. The clouds and sky of the Sound sometimes seem familiar—like those at Devon—and then a white bird will swoop down, and then a whole flock, and there will be such a fecundity of birds that there seems no room for people.

Some of them will not make it; canoes will breach, their sloppy rigging of sails caught in the chop. But Eleanor will make it, and Virginia, and most of the women and children. Flying over the water, looking out from under the patched sails, Eleanor instructs the children to crouch low along the rail so they cannot be seen from shore. Eleanor thinks of this as a Children's Crusade, like that cruel tale of Catholic martyrdom from the distant past. She hopes the children's sweet faces will be their shields against misfortune when they arrive. Until Father can find them and take them back to England. There is no hope in this place, only killing and starvation. Pray it may be better for the children at Chesepiuk.

CROSSING THE GREAT DISMAL SWAMP in an aging Dodge Caravan, it's hard to imagine what it would have been like to walk across it in 1587. The Great Dismal looks pretty tame from the road; there are trash cans and picturesque places to stop and enjoy the creepy green gloom. But pause and peer into the green and there is the water, sluicing dark and mysterious through impenetrable swamp, poisonous vines no doubt dripping with spotted snakes.

You could canoe it. People do it all the time. Indian princess ghosts do it, Bland Simpson, modern-day explorer, author, and songwriter does it. There's even a put-in at the official Dismal Swamp rest area. I recall a canoe trip on the upper Haw River, near the source, where the waterway was narrow and choked with downed trees and vines. We didn't paddle, exactly. We dragged and humped the canoe over obstacles, or slid underneath them, flattening ourselves, face up, to pass under leaning tree trunks encrusted with mud and poison ivy. Our scraping and stumbling passage slowly filled the canoe bottom with shredded vines, spiders, and the occasional watersnake.

I haven't gotten lost yet on this trip so it's about time. I miss my turn, take the next road west and keep going and going. I don't give up until the road turns to a trackless patch of sand in what could very optimistically be described as an abandoned industrial park.

Time to backtrack. I'm late for a date with some bones.

TWO ROANOKE SCHOLARS, Dr. James Kelso and Dr. Nick Luccketti, are working this summer on an archeological study at Jamestown. I've tracked them to Virginia, where the funding pockets seem deeper and the findings have been extraordinary. Archeologists, I'm learning, must be nomads, herding their flocks of graduate students from site to site, depending on the grants they get. It may be a dry season at Roanoke, but here they have unearthed a new cemetery next to James Church, an extraordinary find that gives hope to a continued search for the Lost Ones—if you dig in the right place, you will find what you are looking for.

By the time I make it to Jamestown, it's getting late in the day for archeology—the park office will close in an hour. I ask directions to the digs, and the information lady tells me, "Hurry, they just discovered some new graves." I rush to the site, past the statue of Pocahontas, past the old cemetery and the old church to the newly discovered graves next to the water.

The archeologists have gone off site for the moment, but there is a hubbub in the crowd. The new bones? No, it's the local mystery writer, all in white, pointed trowel in hand, behind the yellow tape that divides the dig from the general public. People are waving books: "Patricia! Patricia!" Someone turns to me and stage-whispers: "That's Patricia *Cornwell*, she's here to do research for her *book*."

I stare down across the barricade: two shallow depressions mark the new find. *There are bones here*, I want to say. *What about the bones?* Patricia ignores the rabble, picks at something with her tool.

"She has a *white helicopter*," someone says. "She flies herself in every day."

I get that sinking feeling that no real conversations will be held within fifty yards of these graves. The archeologists approach. The crowd parts and William Kelso emerges. More waving of books: "Dr. Kelso, Dr. Kelso!" People want him to sign *his* books too. This isn't a dig, it's a book signing.

Turns out there's just been an article in the local paper. It reported that Cornwell is helping fund the dig in exchange for the privilege of getting some background research in for her next book—which will be a *historic* murder mystery. Plenty to work with here, I muse, looking at all the marked squares that were once dead bodies. Eventually I manage to get a word in edgewise: *Dr. Kelso, I want to ask a few questions about your work in Manteo . . .* He kindly refers me to his able colleague, Dr. Luccketti. Once we hike to the new office across the lush green lawn—where indeed Patricia has parked her white helicopter, big as life—we get to have a real conversation.

Luccketti remembers his Roanoke work well. He and Kelso excavated the Roanoke fort in 1994-95, following up on a 1991-93 research project there under archeologist Noel Hume that uncovered "America's first science lab." Centuries of soil disturbance and previous digs had concealed the evidence near the reconstructed earthworks of the fort. The site revealed bricks, chemical glassware, French stoneware flasks, crucible sherds, antimony that was used for assaying metals, and coal and charcoal used for fuel. Thomas Hariot and metallurgist Joachim Gans would have used this lab for testing copper, the primary metal found by Ralph Lane and others among the Indians. They no doubt hoped to assay silver mixed in with the more common metal. Other finds included a fishhook and a lead seal from a bale of cloth, both identifiable as Elizabethan.

For many years, studies of the presumed fort site were frustrated by evidence that the area had been used and re-used and the palisades and various fort structures reconfigured over time. Over the centuries, many others had occupied, surveyed, or excavated the site, including President Monroe, Civil War soldiers, a colony of freedmen, and those who placed a memorial there in 1893 to Virginia Dare, the foundation of which may have destroyed archeological evidence. And though scattered artifacts were sometimes found from the Elizabethan era, there was no compelling pattern of occupation by the colonists, no clear story in the sherds.

In the early 1990s, a startling theory emerged based on artifacts uncovered back in 1982. Evidence of old wooden well shafts had been spotted offshore at low tide, northeast of the fort site. Carbon dating confirmed that the barrel-and-hollow-log construction could have been built by the Roanoke colonists, but no one could figure out what it was doing there in the Sound. At a National Park Service symposium in 1993, Noel Hume suggested that these artifacts might be signs that the village the colonists made was not near the reconstructed fort—that after years of erosion it was now out in the Sound. They had been looking in the wrong place for evidence of the Lost Ones. Or, as Hume quotes archeologist David Phelps as saying, "We have lost the fort and found the colony."[7]

In 1995, Kelso and Luccketti recovered Indian pottery, Spanish olive jar fragments, and flints from the fifteenth to seventeenth centuries at Roanoke. Luccketti wants to go back. Someday he'd like to resurvey a

1940s dig. "We've gotten a lot better at it," he says, "we know more about artifacts and buildings than we used to."

"The English and Spanish records are exhausted," he adds, "but maybe not the Dutch records. We haven't given up hope at Roanoke Island."

In 1996, I learn, David Phelps began a shoreline study of the north end of Roanoke Island, but it had to be put on hold. Later, I will ask him where he thinks the colony village might be found. "It might have been on Dough's Creek," he will tell me. "That would have been a good site for it. Of course that's in the town of Manteo. There's very little undeveloped here by now."

I try to imagine getting permission to dig up one of the carefully tended backyards in the town of Manteo.

———

BEFORE I LEAVE, I manage to get a glimpse of Jamestown bones up close: a man and a woman, faces reconstructed by an artist; a set of long bones lumpy and earth-stained. They had been found laid out flat, in coffins: proper English burials. The man was only about 18, killed by a musket shot to the thigh. The woman was about thirty-five—cause of death unknown. It amazes me that bones last 400 years. Of course I have seen much older relics, in the churches of Rome.

As I stare at the oddly soulless faces of the dead, I consider the bones that lay at my feet an hour before. Who knows who they were? My web research reveals a page telling what to do if you dig up human bones by mistake. Apparently it's not uncommon:

> In North Carolina, many unmarked graves exist without gravestones, fences, tombstones, or other surface indications of their presence. These are chiefly the graves of prehistoric and historic Indians, which may never have been marked at all; and human graves which had been identified at one time in the past, but the markings are no longer visible.[8]

People find bones while building a new house or roadbed. Bones sometimes emerge from the ground, exposed by floodwaters or shifting dunes. Indian bones can be differentiated by the way they are buried: the skeleton is sitting up. I wonder if across the James River somewhere, in the wetlands and swamps, there might be other English bones, as carefully boxed, shrouded, and buried:

> *Scapula, ribcage, spinal column.*
> *Tibia, fibula, skull.*
> *Ivory spars and joints.*
> *Scaffolding for the human spirit.*

At James Church after the tourists go home, things get quiet fast. A shell-pink sky settles over the silky tidewater. A freckled pigeon roosts in the open tower. Inside are plaques and graves, dedicated to everything from Pocahontas to the Tobacco Association. There's a plaque to the Ancient Planters in Virginia:

> Who through evil report
> And loss of fortune
> Through suffering and death
> Maintained stout hearts
> And laid the foundations
> Of our county...

The plaque that captures my imagination, however, is dedicated to George Sandys, American Poet, who

> While Treasurer of the Virginia Colony translated Ovid's Metamorphoses—the first classical work translated on American soil.

It's easy to see the appeal of Ovid in this place. These early colonists, Roanokers and Jamestowners alike, had a tough time wrestling with Fate. Jove was continually sending hurricanes and droughts. Mars was always getting people into wars. (Diana was always sending virgins off into the forest, turning them into white does.) New World living as English people imagined it—shining cities, gold, and acreage—was always morphing into battle and sweat and grubby starvation. Big dreams got reduced to bones and rubble.

I wander along the river into the ruins of the city, square after square of knee-high rock foundation walls that look like they're waiting for the carpenters to show. I settle on a bench. Keeping very still, I see them approach with the dusk: deer, come to graze among the stones.

Chapter 5:

Legendary Roanoke

"I have to teach myself not to read too much into things—it comes from having to read too much into hardly anything at all."
—archeologist character in *The English Patient*, the movie

IN SEPTEMBER, OCTOBER, AND NOVEMBER OF 1999 I will attempt to return to the coast. Like John White, I will be flummoxed by weather: a series of monster storms, one so large it floods all major roads in eastern Carolina for weeks on end. First Hurricane Dennis runs up the Outer Banks, dumps nineteen inches of rain at Ocracoke, cuts a new inlet at Roanoke Island, then turns inland and keeps raining. Hurricane Floyd sweeps inland, dumping twenty inches of rain on saturated ground, drowning fifty-six people. Hurricane Irene glances off the Outer Banks in October, dumping up to ten more inches of rain, prolonging the flooding. Route 64, with all its twists and turns, red wolves and bears, is underwater and stays that way for a long time.

News photos show hundreds of pink pigs congregated on the tin roofs of barns, swimming in brown effluent. Rescue helicopters float over towns and farms moated by a toxic flood. Entire counties retreat to school buildings sited on higher ground and stay marooned for weeks. A friend whose boat I'd hoped to rent reports the beaches of the Outer Banks are littered with the stinking bodies of chickens and turkeys and deer.

Watching East Carolinians tough it out in shelters, taking rescue supplies to my local fire station, I begin to wonder how Native Americans survived hurricanes of this size; I begin to wonder if a similar season left the colonists choked and drowning. I am marooned in Pittsboro; I turn my attention to the written word, the legends and the facts. I am determined, for one, to discover the source of the legend of the white doe. The image evokes a kind of virginal purity reminiscent of unicorns. Perhaps, somewhere, there is documentation of a Native American tradition that will explain how the legend got started.

For enthusiasm, variety, and plain wackiness, F. Roy Johnson's *The Lost Colony in Fact and Legend*[1] is my favorite collection of Colony lore. First Johnson gives the Beechlander legend reported by Victor Meekins, a newspaper editor in Manteo. Eight miles from Roanoke Island, in the middle of a swamp, was a piece of high ground called Beechland, "one of the most secluded places in North Carolina." The settlers cleared several hundred acres of land, fished, grew crops, and hunted for their food. Old-timers told of blue-eyed Indians among the settlers, whose family names were those of Roanokers. "Beechlanders" built two-story houses and buried their dead in coffins made like dugout canoes. So, this is one of the places those colonists could have ended up. I like the name "Beechlander." It doesn't sound like somebody lost.

Other, more ghosty-sounding legends abound. Explorer John Lawson gives an account of local settlers' and Indians' encounters with "Sir Walter Raleigh's Ship," which would appear from time to time. It was under full sail but sailing *against* the wind, a-dazzle with silver light. Others report visions of a Roanoke rescue in the clouds.

At least two tales focus on women: One claims that poor Eleanor, keeping watch for her father by the shore, completely cracked one day and walked into the sea, pursuing a hallucination of his ship; the other reports that Virginia Dare was the real Pocahontas, adopted by Powhatan when he saw her flaxen hair.

In every tale of her I've read, Virginia Dare is described as blonde and pale and beautiful. "She was a babe," one of my archeologist friends jokes. And why not if it makes for a good story? It's the pictures of her with bleached-white, gossamer dresses and perfect curls that get on my nerves. I've heard locals call Virginia "the first *white* child born on American soil," as if the color of her skin might grant her fairytale princess status here. *This ain't Disneyland*, I want to say. I want to tell them her hair would be a *mess* in this climate, and her pale, unprotected skin would be covered in sunburn and mosquito bites. Not to mention the poison ivy.

Johnson's white doe story is credited as "North Carolina's oldest legend," but I don't think any of the sources listed are sixteenth century. In this tale, Manteo ends up raising Virginia as his own daughter, and she becomes the object of affection of both a cute young brave (Okisko) and a nasty old witch doctor (Chico). The magician turns her into a white doe after she rejects him. The white doe haunts the countryside. To turn the spell, Okisko makes a special hoodoo arrow and shoots her. But Chico shoots at the same time, their arrows cross, and just as she is turning back into human form, the second arrow kills her. According to Johnson, the white deer haunts Roanoke Island to this day and leads hunters on a merry chase—only to disappear into the mist at dawn. Okisko, I know from my reading, is the name of a Wepemeoc chief up towards the Chowan River. I haven't read about any Chicos.

Another "Indian" tale: An Occaneechi chief sees young Virginia on a trading mission and falls in love. He takes her home to somewhere on the Eno River near Hillsborough, along with all her people. Other legends make claims for Cedar Island, Gates County, Wilmington, Swain's Mill, and the Lumber River. Along with terrorized colonists, the tales feature Spanish pirates, Tuscarora warriors, and a love child in a blanket left in a pig pen. One seventeenth-century missionary tells of Indians who speak Welsh, have beards, and hoe their crops like Englishmen—descendants of an 1170 voyage, not Roanoke at all. "The chief argument," Johnson says, "against this thesis is that the 'British' language would not have survived over such a long period." But here it is, pushing tendrils out along the borders of probability like that enormous grapevine.

My all-time favorite legend is the "Eleanor Dare Stones," a series of rocks discovered along a trail from North Carolina to Georgia like Hansel and Gretel's breadcrumbs. The surfaces of the stones are carved with messages seemingly from Eleanor Dare to her father John White. Somewhere along the line the stones became a serious subject of study; then they became the subject of ridicule.

The story starts with a traveling salesman: One day in 1937, a businessman stopped along U.S. Highway 117 near Edenton to stretch his legs and quite literally stumbled over a rock with strange inscriptions on it. Irritated and bruised, he tossed the rock into his trunk. Later, he strolled into the alumni hall at Emory University in Atlanta and a great flurry of interest ensued.

Excited about the stone, a part-time professor at Emory named Haywood Pearce, Jr., enlisted his father's aid in purchasing it. Pearce and his father were also vice-president and president of Brenau College, a small Baptist school for women, and they no doubt saw the opportunity to really make a name for their school. The two of them offered rewards for similarly carved stones. More were found. Some of them appeared to be grave markers. Some were carved with newsy notes to John White from his daughter Eleanor, about her travels, her tragedies, her various Indian husbands, and her general well being:

FATHER WEE GOE
SW WITH FOVRE
GOODLIE MEN THEYR SHEW
MOCHE MERCYE...[2]

Locals came forward with inscribed stones that they claimed to have found years before; one stone had been masonry in an old mill, one was found in a ditch next to a plowed field, a trail of them led to a cave whose walls showed a matching inscription. A teenager cracked off pieces of the wall before scholars could see it. Pearce and his father bought land at one of the discovery sites, dug for bones, but found nothing. The cryptic messages, misspelled and roughly carved, gave directions, named colonists, and seemed to express things only colonists would know. The stones listed roster after roster of the dead, felled by Indians or sickness, and the lists of names sometimes matched those on ships' rosters, and sometimes diverged from them. Some theorized that the unknown names were those of Grenville's surviving men, whose identities had not been recorded elsewhere in history.

From Gainesville, Georgia, to the Chattahoochee River, twenty-two stones had been found by 1940; forty-eight were found in all. A mysterious Griffin Jones signed the last stone they found, dated 1599. It tells of the death of his friend Eleanor and the survival of her second daughter, Agnes. The death of Virginia had long since been recorded—on the first rock, along with that of her father, Ananias, and many other colonists.

Georgia residents became inflamed by the idea of finding more stones. Some spent weekends searching for inscribed rocks along the rivers; others created "fake" Dare stones and tried to sell them. By 1940, Pearce was attempting to promote the story of the stones in a play produced at Brenau College, perhaps hoping to capture some of the tourist dollars Paul Green's play had drawn at Manteo. In October of that year, Pearce put a feather in his cap by gaining recommendations from a distinguished group of scholars about how to continue serious study of the stones. Scholars from the Smithsonian found "no evidence of fraud"; they released a statement that the "preponderance of evidence" was that the stones were authentic and deserved study. The Elizabethan language carved on the rocks seemed genuine enough, down to the terrible spelling.

Caught up in his enthusiasm, Pearce wrote a popular article and sent it to the *Saturday Evening Post*, bragging a bit about what he had found. The problem was, there was no proof yet that the stones were authentic, and there were some odd coincidences and conflicts that made them suspect. The *Post* sent out reporter Boyden Sparkes to check up on Pearce's story. First Sparkes conferred with the keepers of the new tourist attraction, the Waterside Theater at Manteo, where *The Lost Colony* played; they heaped scorn on the whole idea. The story of the stones contradicted the history as told in the play; they had very little stake in supporting any new theory. Play promoters were no doubt terrified of losing their paying jobs in the middle of the Depression.

Sparkes dug deep into Pearce's tale and began to interpret it as a hoax. He found much evidence—and may have even made some up, including finding the word "FAKE" inscribed as an acrostic. Sparkes's suspicions focus on the fact that the first stone showed up in 1937, just after the Paul Green play opened, and that the stones found lay in an almost direct line from Edenton, North Carolina—just across the Sound from Manteo—to Atlanta. This meant the discoveries pointed in a persistent line to Pearce's college campus.

Paul Green accused the inscriber of the stones as having "plagiarized at least the framework of my play"—in other words, having stolen the idea of Eleanor as a "pioneering type of woman." Interviewed by Sparkes, Pearce remarked: "If hoax it is, the hoax is more incredible, more fantastic than the story itself."

Meanwhile Hammond, the man who tripped over the first stone, had disappeared from sight. Sparkes hypothesized that Pearce's correspondence with Cecil De Mille (in which he asked the director to consider a local playwright's version of the story for a movie) raised questions that the stones could have been an enormous hoax perpetrated by Hollywood promoters. Sparkes wildly speculated that Hollywood was looking for another blockbuster Southern historical drama on the heels of the success of *Gone with the Wind,* which had just won ten Academy Awards.

In April 1941, instead of publishing Pearce's promotional piece, the *Post* published Sparkes's scathing repudiation. The reporter admitted to resenting the snobbery of the academics about his profession. He picked apart Pearce's writing, paragraph by paragraph, with relish.[3] Sparkes accused Pearce of incompetence—or worse, deliberate promotion of a hoax. He implied there was a conspiracy between Pearce and the "finders" of the stones—a group of woodsmen and moonshiners who lived in tarpaper shacks and had all done time. He described how the rocks could be "faked," and revealed that one of Pearce's woodsmen was known for selling phony Indian relics. An expert was quoted saying that in the Elizabethan age only men of Raleigh's class could write in Roman letters such as were carved on the stones. Everyone else, he said, used "Gothic" letters.

Pearce's career was ruined; the stones were put away; the Smithsonian and other scholars withdrew their interest. Nine months later, the U.S. entered World War II. The country had other things to think about. No excavations have ever been attempted at some of the supposed gravesites. The stones became an embarrassment to historians and archeologists alike, an all-too-close reminder that their hypotheses can be rarely proven, but easily ridiculed.

An article in the *Atlantic*[4] recently noted that in the wake of new field methods, some maverick archeologists are looking anew at certain relics of the ancients in the Americas thought to be hoaxes in the past—the "Norse runes" of Minnesota; the "Hebrew stone" in Los Lunas, New Mexico; the "Iberian carvings" in Grave Creek, West Virginia, among others. The Dare stones merited no mention in the story, perhaps because they are so obscure, just as the colonists' disappearance has been such a dusty story for years. The stones remain at Brenau—all 2,000 pounds of them. Reflecting the wild swings in their status, a few are kept in glass cases on blue velvet in the university archive; most are in storage in a basement room.

Around 1982, a long-haired Leonard Nimoy narrated a wild-eyed docudrama about the stones for his "In Search Of" TV series—a show whose other episodes featured such topics as Bigfoot, Jack the Ripper, the Lost City of Atlantis, and that other mysterious collection of rocks, Stonehenge. In 1991, Robert W. White published a 285-page account of the stones, entitled *A Witness for Eleanor Dare*. He compiled historical material, speculation, and a transcript of the words carved in stone in an attempt to debunk, line for line, the dismissive article published by the *Post*. As far as I can tell, White's impassioned argument has made no difference. The stones remain unstudied and mostly ignored.

It seems fitting that a search for Virginia Dare might end up in a room full of stones with unproven stories meticulously carved on them. If the carvings were a hoax, one has to wonder at the sanity of the rogue who created them. Two thousand pounds of stones. Who could have researched the story, created a plausible narrative, chiseled those rough words all by hand, then dragged them to such remote locations?

I want to go see them for myself.

A dark cellar at the back of some becolumned classroom building in Georgia.
The door opens, letting in a slice of light.
A jumbled mass of brown rocks, the size of my head, the size of small children, piled to the ceiling in the corners, tumbled across the floor like rubble from the Egyptian pyramids.
A monument to the longevity of words carved in stone, whether truth or lies.

There is no white doe in this story; there is only the elusiveness of truth and the power of words—those carved in stone and those printed on paper.

I HEAD TO UNC-CHAPEL HILL hoping scholars there can finally shed light on the white doe story. Someone suggests I speak to Charles Terry Zug, a folklorist who specializes in North Carolina legends. Zug's windowsill gleams with the bared teeth and glaring eyes from a cluster of small brown "face jugs," evidence of one of Zug's passions, folk pottery. The jugs are from a single potter, and all seem intact—in contrast to what may be found *in situ* at Roanoke.

Does Zug think the white doe legend's source is Native American? Not likely, he says. For one, Native peoples simply weren't romantic about relations between men and women. What about women turning into deer and arrow shafts turning into grapevines? What you do if you're a folklorist, he patiently explains, is look up the images in the *Journal of Folk-Motif.* If that image shows up in lots of stories, then look at the tales themselves and see if certain elements in them are repeated.

None of the "legend and lore" books about Virginia Dare give specific sources for the story, but a folklorist would record the name, location, and date of the teller of the tale. Zug suggests that the image of a white doe might show up in European folklore, if not Native American.

Folklore studies once treated their subjects as the Other. Scholars would go into the field, pretend they were being objective, and count and evaluate things and people and behaviors. They often didn't know the language of the cultures they studied. Language contains bias, of course, if only in point of view. These days folklorists are moving toward including themselves as the "I." Even more progressive is the trend toward making studies more like a collaboration with the culture, expressed in a collective point of view.

I wonder if there's ever been a language that did not contain or reflect point of view. I can hardly think about it, not in English anyway; perhaps it would just be something like this: *is, is, is, is, is.*

In UNC's Davis library, there are scads of folklore journals, containing scads of proverbs, Indian tales, and mountain stories. A few of them contain stories about deer. One even has some complication about a black deer, a white deer, and one that's half and half, symbolizing night and day. But none of them relate to Roanoke, and none relate to a romantic story about an English girl whose blonde curls and blue eyes bewitched two Indian men. The folklore search, however unscientific, is a bust.

I catch English professor and writer Bland Simpson in his office, between exams. "Never heard it myself, growing up," he says. As one who mines lore from the Dismal Swamp and eastern Carolina for his books, plays, and music, Simpson would no doubt know such a legend if it were native to his home territory. The experts are beginning to confirm what I can only intuit in my scattershot search: The legend of the white doe was made up, whole cloth, by Sallie Southall Cotten, a Victorian poet who had undoubtedly read too much Longfellow, and who became obsessed with promoting Virginia Dare. Perhaps all too aware, in Reconstruction times, of the presiding idea that North Carolina history was insignificant compared to that of Virginia or South Carolina, Cotten determined to change things. So she wrote a popular poem and performed it, relentlessly, in meeting halls and women's clubs around the country, dressed in a fringed "white deerskin" gown like some vaudeville act out of *Huckleberry Finn*. She printed up handbills to promote her act. She made money from her readings to publish the book. Her preface reads like a political speech. How did she get the idea? What possessed her?

Chapter 6:

The Poetry Lady

O innocent babe! Roanoak's lost nestling!
How shall we learn where thy footsteps did roam?
     —Sallie Southall Cotton,
          The Legend of Virginia Dare

SALLIE SOUTHALL COTTEN, BORN IN 1846 IN VIRGINIA, was educated in North Carolina during the Civil War. She graduated from Greensboro Female College in July 1863, during a time of food shortages and smallpox epidemics. Vicksburg had fallen to the Union and news of Gettysburg and other horrific battles was emerging. At seventeen, the young woman wondered if there would be anyone left to marry; and if not, what kind of life awaited her.

Dependent on a rich relation for her education, she now began to make her way in the world, tutoring and caretaking children until she eventually did marry Robert Cotten in 1866. Neither of them had money or resources. Her husband screwed up his courage, borrowed money from a Yankee former business associate, and started a store. Later they settled at a thousand-acre farm near Greenville on the Tar River. Her scrapbook contains a tiny article lauding her accomplishments years later: "Mrs. Cotten represents the ideal woman of the progressive new South . . ."[1]

Cotten raised six children and ran the household with good cheer and aplomb, creating a school for local children and working to help the local black tenant farmers. In 1883 her oldest son drowned in the Tar

River, on the morning of his fifteenth birthday, and she fell into despondency. In 1890, she moved into a new phase of her life after being invited to act as an "alternate lady manager" at the Chicago World's Fair. The experience would transform her. Having been a leader in her small rural community in the South, Cotten now took on the nation of women as if they were her neighbors. Her journal describes social events with foreign dignitaries' wives, including a tea sponsored by the Queen of Siam. She catches a glimpse of "Mr. Edison," is wowed by the "Moorish Palace" exhibit, but gushes, "to me the Ferris Wheel is the greatest wonder of the Midway."[2]

Sometime between the death of her son and her Chicago experience, Sallie Southall Cotten becomes acquainted with the story of Virginia Dare. She researches the legends about it, makes up an epic poem to honor her, and begins to think of her as a symbolic figure—an "ideal woman" whose image could give others something to aspire to. When it falls to her to gather historical materials and art for an exhibit about colonial North Carolina, she dives into the job with enthusiasm. She tracks down a painting of the "Edenton Tea Party," in which Carolina lady revolutionaries protested British colonial rule. Cotten finds relics to display from a Bertie County Indian Mound. Then she tackles the problem of how to properly honor Virginia Dare.

She commissions a desk, hand carved in white holly with scenes showing what Dare's life might have been. She negotiates to buy a statue of Dare by a Miss Maria Louisa Lander. She makes plans to ring the Fair's Columbian Peace Bell on August 18, to celebrate Dare's birthday. "If it is done," she writes, "Virginia Dare will no longer be forgotten by Americans." Somewhere along the line she has become obsessed with America's first missing child.

Sallie Cotten goes home lit up, ready to organize a local federation of women's clubs and raise money for two pet projects—a Virginia Dare vocational school for women and a Virginia Dare Memorial Association. Her method of fundraising will move from selling hooked rugs to giving speeches to performing her own epic poem on stage.

Completed sometime before 1897, not published until 1901, Cotten's *The Legend of the White Doe* is the maddeningly sentimental work of a deeply intelligent Victorian writer. Its stanzas are a feast of predictable rhythms and rhymes whose cadences awkwardly strive toward the hypnotic sounds of Longfellow's *Hiawatha*, but miss them by a long shot. Cotten's imagery is lush and sometimes inventive, but the story itself seems melodramatic to the modern sensibility honed on irony.

Especially sentimental is the cover of the "souvenir edition," printed in 1937 by the Roanoke Island Historical Association. Here again—this time embellished in color—is that blonde-coifed, misty-eyed maiden with the pink ribbon in her bonnet who graces bottles of sweet Virginia Dare wine. A frontispiece shows a kind of ideal woman, in balletic pose, draped in white doeskin in the forest primeval.

Sallie Southall Cotten had an agenda in writing and promoting this work, that much is clear. She intended to elevate the cause of North Carolina women, raise money for her school, and gain a rightful place for Virginia Dare in the annals of history. In the first goal, she succeeded; in the second goal, she was derailed. While she was in Chicago, the state of North Carolina finally established a vocational school for women but did not name it for Dare. As far as Dare's place in history—well, her story still seems dusty and obscure a century later, but one wonders if we would remember it at all if not for her poem and Paul Green's play.

Cotten's letters reveal her complex mind. A product of the antebellum South, she writes equally convincingly of organizing a hog killing and organizing the women of America. Her letters reveal her nature to be a confounding mix of progressive and racist, sardonic and hopelessly romantic. She is an admirer of Jane Addams' progressive Hull House; she is a plantation wife and mother of nine, six surviving. She is an unreconstructed Southern Democrat who believes in states' rights and the nobility of the Cause; she is also an apologist for Negro rights in the legislature—her convictions stemming from a sense of duty in being part of a "superior race." She is a severe critic of white Republicans who schmooze Negro votes but don't invite them to their inaugural balls. She is also a voracious reader of sentimental poetry.

Somehow she got the idea that Virginia Dare could beat Pocahontas in a fistfight if she had to. Infuriated at the sight of Pocahontas prominently displayed in the American history frieze in the U.S. capitol rotunda—and no mention of Dare—Cotten doggedly determined that someday a statue of Virginia would be placed in an equally prominent location, perhaps the Hall of History in Raleigh, if she had anything to say about it.

I am surprised by Cotten's letters; they show humor, wit, and a wacky genius bordering on the prescient. I keep leafing back in time for letters that may speak to how she got the idea for the poem—where, indeed, did she hear the story of the white doe? In 1897 she was fifty-one, up to her neck in national women's movement activities and performing "The White Doe" publicly at commercial poetry readings. The money she made from such readings would pay for printing the book itself. Forty years after slave poet George Moses Horton was selling his poems to buy his freedom in Chapel Hill, Cotten was selling her performances in order to change the world. Being a poet in the nineteenth century wasn't all poverty and angst. There was apparently some cash involved.

Cotten performed at theaters as well as women's clubs, though sometimes she found it hard to get a commercial booking, for the local "popular cheap rate troupe" had snagged all the dates. She laments, after losing a performance opportunity: "Thus the hand of destiny is upon me for daring to molest a subject upon which the fate of obscurity and oblivion already rested… I took interest and pleasure in writing 'The White Doe,' and now it is completed I am content to abide and await further developments." She confesses to feeling "a little cynical to-night." A postscript reveals she is reading a book called *The Sorrows of Satan*, which may account for her depressed mood.[3]

I read packet after packet of letters, but cannot find any clues to where the idea for her "White Doe Legend" came from. Who told her this preposterous tale? Or did she simply make it up? I open another packet of papers to discover a carefully pasted scrapbook, less than half full. Its first pages are crammed with clippings of poetry from magazines and newspapers, most of them unattributed and undated. On some pages, she has marked out a poem's cadence, as if she were studying up for her epic-to-come. Many clippings involve dead babies or angelic children and dear, sweet, tiny baby clothes. A few are word games— notably, a poem that consists of the same words repeated in each line, in different order and with different punctuation: "The weary plowman plods his homeward way. / Weary, the plowman plods his way homeward," etc.

One unattributed piece, called "The Long Ago," seems to capture her feelings about the uses of history for Victorian romantics:

> *Ah! every heart holds some sweet dream*
> *Of the days that have gone before.*

Several "Indian legends" fit into those pages, along with tiny scraps of infinitesimal print about the healing properties of precious gems, and ballads to John Wilkes Boothe and other Confederate heroes. I find pictures of woman doctors and a stern looking character, Belva A. Lockwood, "the first woman to run for president of the United States." Loosened from its page, a portrait of Lincoln falls into my hand.

In a "line a day" book, a gift from namesake daughter Sallie for Christmas after the turn of the century, Cotten writes what might be a prose poem in the flyleaf:

> *Grief is a month of sobs & tears;*
> *Sorrow is a dear memory buried away and taken out at times*
> *to caress and cry over;*
> *a tragedy is a hurt that leaves a scar on the soul.*
> *Scars last until death,*
> *and pale and burn under strong emotion.*

She signs it "Mrs. Cotten." Who knows what she was thinking of? Perhaps her son Robbie, who drowned back in 1883, or one of her other dead children. She does not say.

On June 13th, 1897, Cotten reports to a young cousin that she does public work out of a sense of obligation: "I do not seek it, nor care for it, but when it comes to me as an opportunity to help prepare my sister women for the future, which is full of opportunities and dangers for them, I feel that it is my duty to do what I can. Especially as I do seem to be somewhat adapted to it and it comes easy to me to do, what many seem too timid to undertake."

When *The White Doe* was finally published, its title page bore the following ambiguous phrasing:

The White Doe
THE FATE OF
VIRGINIA DARE
An Indian Legend
By Sallie Southall Cotten

Does Cotten's careful phrasing imply that she made up an Indian Legend? It almost sounds that way. The mind casts back to that plowman poem—the way words are placed makes a difference. The White Doe is both a book and a legend—an Indian legend—by Sallie Cotten. I realize that I don't know: Is Hiawatha a legend or a fiction, in poem form, by Longfellow? I look it up: Longfellow stole Indian tales from Henry Schoolcraft's ethnographies.[4] He took poetic license, mixing up Iroquois and Chippewa hero-and-devil tales and getting the whole thing appallingly wrong—which didn't seem to bother most readers.

Cotten claims historical antecedent for her work, however:

> This tradition of a white doe and a silver arrow has survived through three centuries, and not only lingers where the events occurred, but some portions of it are found wherever in our land forests abound and deer abide. From Maine to Florida lumbermen are everywhere familiar with an old superstition that to see a white doe is an evil omen....That such a creature as a white deer really exists is demonstrated by their capture and exhibition in menageries, and to-day the rude hunters of the Allegheny Mountains believe that only a silver arrow will kill a white deer.[5]

I can attest to the existence of white deer myself. For two hunting seasons, my neighbor Grady kept me informed of the movements of a white deer that roamed the woods and fields near my farm. Local hunters were tracking it. There seemed to be a frenzy of hunters one fall, boldly pursuing their prey without respect for boundaries. One fall day as I dozed under a favorite tree, I heard rustling through leaves scant yards from where I sat. A poacher had jumped a fence and was cutting across my neighbor's field, loaded gun pointing in my direction. On my early morning walks, I saw trucks with empty gun racks parked on the power line right-of-way. I thought of placing spikes under their tires, but perhaps I didn't need to. Grady always sent them in the wrong direction.

Long before I ever heard of Sallie Cotten, the idea of a white deer fired my imagination. I looked for it on my walks. One foggy morning Grady passed me in his truck, stopped, and backed up very slowly. He rolled down his window and whispered "It's back there, at the power line. Just standing there. Go get a look." It was gone by the time I got there, a wisp of white bounding over the hill.

A few days later someone came into the store where I worked downtown and told me, "Somebody shot the white deer. He's getting a picture taken for the paper." I felt an unaccountable rage. I ran outside. "Where did you shoot that deer?" I asked, accusingly. He wasn't telling. The picture was in the paper, carcass hanging from a rope.

The hunter had the animal stuffed and its eyes set with glass. For a long time it stood in the corner of the Citgo on the way to Jordan Lake. Everyone seemed to think it was good luck, and everyone but me and Grady seemed to like it being dead—I guess because you could touch it any time you wanted, instead of having it vanish into mist. Neighbors and friends talked at the store—turns out there are lots of white deer in Chatham County. There's a whole race of them, some mutant gene pool. I've seen one in Pittsboro, crossing a side road down by Robeson Creek. There's even a legendary white doe of Fearrington Village that passes, wraithlike, among suburban houses of an evening. Still, I've never heard anybody around here bring up Virginia Dare when a white deer passes by. It's awfully far from Manteo.

Has everyone who knew the legend of the white doe died? Is it a closely held secret, kept by the tight-lipped people of East Carolina for lo these many years? Knowing a few East Carolinians, I can't believe it. Those people *love* to tell stories. Did entire nations of Native Americans die with their lips sealed? Did all of the keepers of local legends and tales—the Walsers and Johnsons and Whidbees—who scooped up whatever scraps of legend they could find and wrote them down, come up completely empty-handed when in came to Indian sources for this tale? I have found folktales for white-footed horses, peacocks, lighthouses, whiskey, and a suicide train. I have found proverbs about the devil beating his wife and the rain crow, and about witching people with crosses marked in the road. I have found Indian princess stories involving riddles that sound just like Grimm's fairy tales. Here's what I found about deer, period:

> *A pain on the left side is a sign to the hunter that he will kill a doe on the morrow.*[6]
> *Whistle to a deer and he will stop.*[7]

I have asked students, scholars, strangers in bars, guys in boatyards, and a homeless man hanging out near the dock in Swansboro. I have asked hunters in trucks, the Wildlife Commission, friends on the phone, and old men standing in line at the McDonald's in Manteo. I have checked folklore journals for North Carolina and Indian legends of the Algonquians. An eclectic survey indeed, but with one consistent result: nobody ever heard of it. They've heard of blue-eyed Indians though. For sure there are blue-eyed Indians.

Whether the source is Indian totemic legend, romantic exaggeration, bastard Ovid, or bad Longfellow, Cotten's white doe legend has a certain appeal: it has sex (or at least arousal), evil, death, and transformation. As there are no suitably bizarre scholarly theories of how the legend came to be, I feel free to promote several of my own: I say this is Sallie Cotten's resurrection story, perhaps an unwitting reference to her Christian/pro-woman beliefs. By masking her thinking in the cloak of heathen legend, Cotten has revealed her own sense of things: Women can transform the world; lust breeds violence; women can rise again in mythic forms (white deer, grapevines) and overwhelm, then civilize, the world of men. Virginia Dare is her Christ figure, out of place in the world, converting the savage heart with an incomprehensible purity. The two arrows converging are her cross; the white doe sightings are Him risen. The vine is the Christian church, flowering in the adversity of a corrupted world.

The truth is, I have felt a discomfiting identification with Cotten. My imagination has filled in gaps that open on the pages of her letters. What is there for me to identify with in a Southern plantation lady? I live in this part of the South for its landscape's promise of sweetness; she seems to love her farm. I lost one child, she lost several. I turned to community work, quite consciously, to distract myself; she sweeps the nation with speeches and keeps a scrapbook of poems about dead babies. I spy footpaths of depression and grief—notes in the margins, long sighs, inexplicable moods—trailing off from all her cheerful forward motion. She promotes the abused and forgotten Virginia Dare as a political banner for the women of America, their purity and power. Perhaps she thinks of Virginia as a lost daughter. Having lived through Reconstruction, poverty, and making her way in the world alone, Sallie Cotten may have felt a twinge of identification with Dare—a babe in the wilderness.

Oddly, sitting in the UNC-Chapel Hill Manuscripts Collection with my pencil and Sallie Cotten's memorabilia, I am reminded of my grandmother. As one who concealed all relation to Confederate heroes, she has no place here, no affinity with Cotten—except perhaps in the clear-eyed dignity and ladylike carriage shown in old photographs. It's absurd. Perhaps the scent of old wood or paper or books brings a connection so visceral. Like the time I sneaked into my grandmother's bathroom and sprinkled her tooth powder on my tongue, I can taste something mysterious and forbidden. When I lived in her house, I became attached to her things: touching them made the mystery of my grandmother more real. I dream of her house with astonishing regularity.

It's not surprising her house would show up in my dreams: I dream of houses obsessively. I dream of abandoned villas by the sea, room after room painted with sunset, floorboards sagging, windows so big you could fall out of them. I dream of condos: my worst nightmare. Room after room painted beige, a shotgun kitchen leading to a narrow squeeze of yard, a distant view to a castle in a field full of horses. I dream of mansions, church walls, apartment buildings, and log cabins. Then there is the dream of my grandmother's house.

My family lived with my grandmother when I was between the ages eight and eleven. Perhaps these are the years when the imagination is most impressionable, seeking to connect the inner life with the outer world. I spent those years reading through the local library's shelf of fairy tales—the *Pink Fairy Book*, the *Green Fairy Book*, the *Blue Fairy Book*—and all the dog and horse stories I could lay my hands on. Horses were completely imagined beings for me, but dogs—forbidden then in grandmother's carefully tended yard—were known objects of great affection. My best friend and I rescued a lost collie pup from the park and returned it to kindly elderly neighbors. They invited us to visit our new dog friend, and themselves, just a few blocks away from my grandmother's house. I allowed myself to imagine what it would be like to be their adopted grandchild—playing with collies in the yard, having tea and cookies, having a grandmother who baked and wore aprons and let me sit in her lap. I was far too timid to pursue this friendship.

My friend returned to her Barbies and I returned to books. I read Robert Louis Stevenson, slipped from the shelf of matching leather-bound classics. I read C. S. Lewis's Narnia stories, about children escaping to magical lands, ruled by a kindly lion, and wept when the spells did not work for me. I spent the summers playing under what we knew as the "largest star magnolia in Washington D.C." And I spent the springs attempting to lure dogs and cats into the yard through the picket fence.

The dream of my grandmother's house is so vivid that I always wake believing the house has a secret, narrow, back stairwell. I peer upward to the crazy slant of treads, the angle of light going to someplace unknown. Sometimes I make it halfway up. I rarely remember what is at the top. The secret stairs are my own invention—truer, perhaps, than the mortal frame of the house. But my grandmother's house was full of real sensual treasures as well: the smell of bananas and old wood; the soft felt key pads and long harp-like strings inside the baby grand piano; the ebony sheen and exotic curve of the piano body; the rich red weave of the Oriental carpet underneath.

A white china cat, with green glass eyes, deliciously cool and smooth to the touch.
A glass candy dish topped by a brass stag.
Corner cupboards filled with china figures.
A breakfast nook with tropical birds painted on the walls.

The house was fancier than any place I'd lived before. But there were secrets: we weren't allowed into my grandmother's room. A recent widow, working for her living, she was scarcely there. There was my father's attic study he crept to in the middle of the night, up a narrow stair to write books and study Russian. There were summer nights at my bedroom window watching fireflies' secret signals in shades of gold and green. There was the garden, full of perennials that swelled out of the earth in spring like alien beings. Pink and tender they emerged from the soil, one day uncurling in a profusion of shapes and colors: airy coral bells, gold forsythia wands, tiger lilies, and my favorite, the tight-budded, ant-covered peony with its wedding-dress bloom.

There were mysteries on the city sidewalks—surveyors' marks we called monkey paws, which had to be jumped over. There were large, dark women who brooded on street corners where we waited for the bus. One early summer morning, when the busy city street we lived on was deserted, my sister and I ran out on a dare and stood there, for an instant, holding hands, amazed and thrilled to our bones that we were not immediately run over. Summer brought an eclipse, when all the leafy shadows multiplexing the sidewalk turned into half moons, then slivered away in darkness.

I think my grandmother was the biggest mystery of all. In the three years we lived in the same house I was terribly afraid of her, for no good reason. She kept to herself. I could not understand her, because I did not know her. My sister and I hid in the basement playing wholesome games in the dark, out of her way.

I found out later she had her losses: a beloved brother who died young; a breakdown after childbirth; a sister she sometimes fought with. In her retirement, I sought out her friendship on a few rare occasions. I took walks with her on country roads, and she told me family stories, though they raised more questions than answers. One day, as if revealing all her secrets at once, she lifted her blouse and showed me fat black moles covering her torso, like a warning or a family curse—something I apparently may inherit. All I really comprehended of her nature was her garden, its profusion and steady bloom. I have planted perennials around my house in homage to her steadfast nurture of beautiful things.

It did not occur to me till later—when my world view had expanded enough to allow older people to have lives and secrets of their own—that during those years she was living a secret life in her own house. Still grieving her husband, she lived in a house invaded by boisterous children.

She escaped to her solitude, her garden. Long after my family had a house of its own, and I had grown up to make a life of my own, my grandmother sold the house and garden. I would drive through the alley late at night, after the bars closed, and spy on what remained. When the enormous yard was sold for a condominium lot, I remember the gaping and perfectly square hole dug in the earth for its foundation. It was like a grave for a whole townful of people.

When I dream of her garden, however, it is how I want it to be, fecund and bellowing with colors.

Sallie Cotten's life, splayed out before me in her private papers, breaks open a complete stranger and her secrets. Though she and my grandmother inhabited completely different worlds, though their generations are separated by more than fifty years, imagination has been at work, drawing parallels, fitting knowledge against yearning, inhabiting a character. I have been pretending I know Sallie Cotten. I have caught myself pretending she is my grandmother.

THE STORY OF VIRGINIA DARE IS A FAMILY STORY—full of high hopes, untold stories, disconnection. In the wake of the Disney's recent Pocahontas movies, with their attendant action figures and CD sing-along soundtracks, and the wonderfully sensuous Pocahontas romance *The New World*, it does seem unfair that Virginia Dare never got her due in the national imagination. Tucked into the first edition of *The White Doe* I find a yellowed, typed section of onionskin, containing an outline for a movie. Sallie Cotten was making a bid for fifteen minutes of fame for her Virginia:

> Reel 1 might open with the pictures of Sir Walter Raleigh and Queen Elizabeth. Then a Court Scene showing Elizabeth on the throne giving unto the hand of Sir Walter Raleigh the Letters Patent of the new lands he was supposed to colonize.
>
> Next picture might show the Indians on shore holding a High Feast and dancing—with gourd rattle and appropriate symbols introduced.[8]

80

A silent movie about the Lost Colony was made in 1921, but I've never seen it. I don't know if this script was used. An agency turned Cotten's story down—it had just decided to make a movie about Jamestown.

What strikes me about Cotten's script is this: Those first two sketches bear close resemblance to scenes in Paul Green's play.

I leave the library discouraged, promising myself I will return and try again. I have not found what I was looking for; I have found something else entirely.

WHEN I DO RETURN, I find page after page of genealogy, tracing the Southall family back to the early 1700s, to Ireland like my father's father. Cotten's hand has sketched out the lives of individuals from the past, each on his or her own page. There is an astonishing story about a freed slave, a former African prince who convinces the Cotten family to return him to his people. There is a series of annual journals, the size of prayer books, bound in brown paper and tied with red ribbon. Each was apparently written after the fact: "Events in the Life of Sallie Southall Cotten during the year 1913," and so on. It is as if she expected the journals to be discovered and read after she was buried—and intended the world should finally understand her properly.

This is just the sort of thing one wishes John White had had the presence of mind to deliver to the future; this is the kind of thing I wish my own father would write, perhaps without the self-conscious presentation and pretty ribbons. It occurs to me that despite all this careful packaging, the world has not beat a path to Cotten's papers; the only current biography I have found of this fascinating, infuriating Victorian is out of print.

Here also I find a twenty-year struggle to bring Maria Louisa Lander's Virginia Dare statue to North Carolina. Cotten finally convinced Lander to donate the statue to the state. It stands nowadays on Roanoke Island amid the plantings and statuary of the Elizabethan Gardens, within reach of tangled vines and live oaks. It is as obscure as the little book Sallie Cotten believed would make us cherish Virginia Dare—first daughter, first mother, ideal woman, ghost.

LANDER'S DARE STATUE SUFFERED ITS OWN DRAMATIC SWINGS OF FATE. The sculptor, from Salem, Massachusetts, worked in Rome in the mid-nineteenth century. Over a period of fourteen months in her Italian studio, Lander carved Virginia's semi-nude form in fine white Carrara marble, Michelangelo's favored material. Some have speculated that Lander had Botticelli's painting "Birth of Venus" as her model. Virginia stands naked to the waist and draped in fishnet, with a companion heron at her feet and Native ornaments detailing her arms and throat. On its way home to Boston the finished figure went down in a shipwreck off the coast of Spain and sunk to the bottom of the sea. A salvage crew dragged it up intact several years later and sold it back to Lander.

Finally bought by a collector in New York, the "Dare Venus" again faced destruction, this time by fire. The statue survived, but the new owner died shortly thereafter, and again the figure reverted to Lander. Perhaps believing fate had a hand in keeping them together, Lander grew quite attached to her "Virginia." She did not attempt to part from her creation again until 1893, when she wrote to Sallie Cotten at the North Carolina Commission for the Chicago World's Fair, offering to sell it for the exhibit. Lack of funding stymied the effort, but Cotten eventually persuaded Lander to donate the statue to the state of North Carolina after her death.

How did Cotten finally persuade her? She traveled to Lander's home, then in Washington, D.C., where the statue was displayed in a bay window of the sitting room. Lander was in the habit of greeting her creation each morning, as the pure white stone gathered the eastern light: "You look beautiful this morning, Virginia," Lander would say. Cotten did not find this extraordinary. She proceeded to don her white fringed gown and perform her entire "White Doe" to an audience of two: the artist and her sculpture. Lander was wowed. Here was a woman whose obsession matched her own.

In 1926, a few years after Lander's death, the "Dare Venus" went on display at the Hall of History in Raleigh, under the portraits of several Confederate heroes, where it suffered vandals and complaints about obscenity. By 1938 the statue had fallen out of favor. It was left in storage in the basement of the old supreme court building, followed by a stint in the state auditor's office. When Paul Green's play was produced at Manteo, the statue was shipped to the Waterside Theater for display there. But again the figure was deemed inappropriate—this time by Park Service historians. Because they had no evidence that Virginia Dare had lived to maturity, the statue stayed in its crate backstage. Sometime after World War II the theater manager sent the statue to Paul Green's estate in Chatham County—just up the road from me. Again, it never came out of its box.

Finally, almost a hundred years after it first took form, the statue took its place at the Elizabethan Gardens, created in Manteo in 1951 by the Garden Clubs of North Carolina. Now the Dare Venus holds court near the wild edges of the formal paths, within spitting distance of the shushing tide of Albemarle Sound. Shipwrecked, abandoned, reviled, and ignored, Lander's "Virginia Dare" suffered a fate that almost mirrors the fate Cotten feared for the "first English child in America."

Chapter 7:

In Greenville

*History with its flickering lamp stumbles along the trail
of the past, trying to reconstruct its scenes, to revive its
echoes, and kindle with pale gleams the passion of
former days.*

> —Winston Churchill, from a
> tribute to Neville Chamberlain

DECEMBER 10, 1999. Route 64 is finally clear of flood debris. At the
crack of dawn I head to the campus of East Carolina University in
Greenville, home of two of the best sources of contemporary research
about the Lost Colony. The Phelps Archeology Lab—now headed by
Dr. Charles Ewen—was named for its founder, archeologist David Phelps.
Now retired from the ECU faculty, Phelps continues to conduct research,
including the digs at the Buxton site on Hatteras Island. Some of his
finds will be here at the lab. Perhaps I'll even get a glimpse of the Kendall
ring. I'll also visit the Roanoke Colonies Research Office, headed by
English professor E. Thomson Shields. It is a repository for written
materials of all kinds on the subject of the Lost Ones. I hope to track
down some elusive papers from a conference about the Roanoke colony.

The road passes through barren country and I scout for signs of the
recent devastation. The ditches are dry, the fields covered in the detritus
of last year's crops. Downtown Rocky Mount and Tarboro seem
remarkably unscathed. Near Greenville, fields sprout with new trailer
cities: temporary housing for those who have lost everything.

PHELPS ARCHEOLOGY LAB. I walk into a large room littered with potsherds, animal bones, and deer teeth on every flat, white surface. The potsherds all appear to be approximately the same size, color, and shape. To a layperson's eye, they look like pieces of an enormous, room-sized jigsaw puzzle, no clue to how they fit. It's a wonder anyone can put them together and make sense of them. In a raised, waist-level box of sand there it is: Half a Colington pot, unglazed, brown clay, its outer surface impressed with woven patterns. This came from the Hatteras site. Next to it on a table, another pot, more fully constructed, from a Tuscarora site. I can't tell the difference.

It's a good thing I have a tour guide: Dr. Charles Ewen begins to explain what is laid out before me. Every sherd, constructed or loose, is labeled in tiny black lettering along one edge. The inside of the Colington pot reads like a book of code. The "Colington period," in archeological parlance, refers to the culture of Algonkian Indians from AD 800 to AD 1650, which includes the time period of the Roanoke colony. Who knows? This pot may have been used by Croatoan people in the time of Manteo.

Nearby lies a stack of plastic sandwich bags, also meticulously labeled. One says "31Dr1 Acc. No. 1283"—the "31" is a code for North Carolina, the "Dr" means Dare County, and the "1" means the first site recorded in Dare County. Another bag contains a flake of blue-white glazed porcelain, too small to code. It is Delftware made in the Netherlands, fifteenth to seventeenth century. The next baggie contains a chunk of clay about the heft and color of a bite from a Mrs. Fields chocolate cookie. It's from a Spanish olive jar. Olive jars didn't just contain olives, Ewen points out. Like the Roman amphoras of old, people used them for everything.

As my eye adjusts to the profusion of objects, the potsherds and artifacts from the Buxton site begin to fall into simple patterns of division: European and non-European. Animal and human. Here is an odd-shaped piece about the size of a finger: a knife blade, swollen with oxidation. Here is a smooth white clay tube: an English pipe stem. Here is the jawbone of a deer. The archeologists have uncovered a village occupied by both Croatoan and Englishman. The trick seems to be figuring out who was there when, and not getting things mixed up. Archeologists are incredibly good at this, and getting better at it all the time.

The Buxton site was first explored about fifty years ago by archeologist William Haag. In 1993, local residents noticed erosion from Hurricane Emily had uncovered a new layer of Croatoan village. In March 1996, David Phelps reported new findings and called it "the most important site on the Outer Banks—and one of the most significant in the mid-Atlantic region."[1] The dig is located at the spot where sixteenth-century maps placed the village of Croatoan, where Manteo and his people lived. In 1998 the Kendall signet ring was found.

"That's the cool find," Ewen says. I agree. But I'll have to talk to Phelps to find out more.

We retreat to Ewen's office for coffee. Over his desk is a velvet Elvis, a favorite cultural artifact. This archeologist's sense of history embraces more than potsherds. "You know about the really coolest find about the colony?" he grins. "The Eleanor Dare stones!" We both laugh. Years ago Ewen studied the Kensington Rune Stone in Minnesota—a carved rock, long considered a hoax, that supposedly was left behind by Viking explorers. The Rune Stone is being reconsidered by modern-day scholars. Like me, Ewen wouldn't mind getting a look at the Dare stones; they have their appeal, whether you believe in them or not.

———

I AM ABLE TO TRACK PHELPS DOWN BY EMAIL. He reports back that the Kendall ring was found in the course of normal excavations in one of the squares near the seventeenth-century workshop area. The site is under the old town of Buxton and had been relatively undisturbed. The ring was found in a stratum for the period between 1625 and 1750. "It had been used so long the shank was worn through and broken," he reports.

Phelps says the College of Arms in London confirmed that the lion symbol on the ring is the Kendall family crest. Like lebame houston, Phelps believes the ring most likely belonged to Master Kendall, a member of Ralph Lane's expedition in 1585-86. Lane's men had much contact with the village of Croatoan, some even lived there for a time. The ring could have been lost there, given as a gift, or traded. "In either case," Phelps says, "the ring ties Croatoan to the Roanoke colonies."

There's a much more recent find however. Just last month, in

November 1999, Phelps found "a snaphaunce-type flintlock" of a sort first used in 1630. Other finds dating from 1655 to 1680 include gun flints, both English and Native-made; iron tools; glass beads; copper and brass fragments and artifacts; two copper farthings from the reign of King George II; and a bale seal with the king's mark. Shell beads, bone ring beads, Colington pottery, European pottery, and other artifacts too numerous to mention have also been recovered. In addition, there is much evidence to show that the Croatoan were producing lead shot from molds in their workshop. European and Croatoan people interacted far beyond the time of the Roanoke colonies.

Two Indian burials have been found, both from after 1650. No English, so far.

I remember a glimpse of oblong boxes, carefully shelved in a special room back at the lab. "Human bones," Ewen told me.

So does Phelps think Virginia Dare went to Croatoan? "I follow David Quinn's theory that the Lost Colony went on to Chesapeake where they had planned to go," Phelps says. "The fact that 'Croatoan' was carved on the gatepost at the Cittie of Ralegh may indicate that a few went to Croatoan village to await White's return. Or it could mean that the whole colony went there temporarily. Virginia Dare was most probably among them."

DR. E. THOMSON SHIELDS TEACHES COLONIAL AMERICAN LIT and runs the Roanoke Colonies Research Office. Though it is housed in Shields' office in the Department of English, RCRO was created in 1993 as a clearinghouse for information about Roanoke from many disciplines, including anthropology, American studies, archeology, biology, history, geography, literature, and Native American studies. Shields is working with Ewen to publish the papers from a recent Roanoke Colony conference that spans all these areas of study.[2]

On a bookshelf in his office sits a world globe the size of your hand, a copy of *Blue Highways*, a row of Tony Hillerman paperbacks, and two volumes of the *Secret Diary of William Byrd of Westover*. The latter was recently decoded from the author's eighteenth-century encryption, Shields explains. I try to imagine writing my entire life story in secret code.

The next two shelves are crammed with books on Virginia Dare and the "Lost Colony" ranging from the ridiculous to the sublime.[3] Shields starts pulling out his favorites. A beautiful Indian maiden graces the cover of the paperback novel *Jamestown* by Angela Elwell Hunt. The novel is the sequel to *Roanoke, The Lost Colony,* her "Christian romance" about the fate of Eleanor Dare's red-headed cousin Jocelyn. I scanned this at the Wilson library back in Chapel Hill. I remember Jocelyn's main concern is: Will she ever have sex with her angst-ridden preacher husband? I flip through the *Jamestown* sequel. Pocahontas figures prominently. On page 162, she runs slam into Jocelyn's husband, the incorrigibly unsexy Rev. Whitaker, who tells her, "Give your pain to God, Pocahontas."

Another paperback cover shows a dignified-looking Indian chief of unknown origin under the legend *Tunkashila: From the Birth of Turtle Island to the Blood of Wounded Knee.* "Boy Scouts around the campfire," Shields says. The word "tunkashila" is defined as "the history of the world as told by a stone." Somewhere near the back of the book—after Chief Seattle's famous rant—is the legend of the white doe. Undoubtedly drawn from Sallie Cotten's work, the story is repeated as authentic Indian legend (her claim also), but given no source. In a widening gyre of imagination and documentation, Sallie Cotten's nineteenth-century epic poem is thus authenticated, in a late twentieth-century paperback, as a sixteenth-century Indian legend. Shields says the true origins of the story are in England; it is fascinating to see it transferred to North America and made into Native lore.

Shields says he and his colleague Charles Ewen have a running joke going: Ewen says that he bases his hypotheses on *provable facts*, unlike his colleagues in the English Department, who don't care what's true or not, as long as it makes a good story.

There is a modern interest, Shields says, in reporting the Roanoke story from the Native American point of view. A scholar has recently written a doctoral thesis in that vein about the battle over the stolen silver chalice that resulted in Ralph Lane's destruction of an Indian village.[4]

Then there is Robert W. White's fantastic, passionately researched account of the "Dare stone" story, *A Witness for Eleanor Dare.* "It reads well," Shields admits, "until you figure out about halfway through what White's theory is: *the stones must be real because there are so many of them.*" Shields' favorite aspect of the story concerns the motives of Haywood Pearce, Jr., the scholar who first latched on to them. He points out that Pearce, as a nontenured history professor, was no doubt desperate to make a name for himself and make his career.

In addition to all these fantastic tales Shields keeps a running bibliography of published and unpublished papers relating to all the Roanoke voyages going back to 1729. The last decade lists more than ninety items, on subjects from Native American resurrection myths to Sir Francis Drake.

What really happened to the Lost Colony? Surely with all his access to research, Shields has a good guess.

"I heard a writer in an interview once," he says, "who told about an experience he had promoting his book in towns all over eastern North Carolina. He said that in every town someone would always pull him aside and say, 'I know where the Lost Colony went.' And he would say, 'Where?' and they would say, 'Here.'"

"So," Shields grins broadly, "we can conclude that the 'Lost Colonists' probably split up, each going to a different town!"

How does our resident expert feel about the Manteo official who claimed that Shakespeare wrote *The Tempest* about the Lost Colony? There are certainly similarities: The spirit-infested island, the shipwrecked father and daughter, the howling storm, the approach of rescue ships— or enemies. Shields says it's not likely. Rather, most scholars believe that *The Tempest* was written on the heels of the founding of Jamestown. One of the ships heading there was shipwrecked near Bermuda. Survivors made it home to England and published widely circulated pamphlets about their ordeal. So, again Jamestown wins—it's got Pocahontas, it's got Shakespeare, it's got novelists with white helicopters . . .

But Roanoke has Sallie Cotten and those Dare Stones.

So many of White's and Hariot's papers and drawings were lost. So much remains unexplained. People will write stories. They'll make them up, out of facts, legends, significant details, images and artifacts. They'll wrap the story in their own feelings and prejudices about human nature, and make a "brave new world, that has such people in it."

I AM DETERMINED TO FOLLOW SHIELDS' ADVICE and take a look at an early edition of *Hakluyt's Voyages*[5] he says is kept in ECU's Joyner Library. During the sixteenth century Hakluyt published the reports and maps of English explorers and adventurers from all over the world, including those of Hariot and White. Even the late editions I have been consulting seem fragile with age. To touch a first edition would be something.

Inside the stacks, a blue neon squiggle lights the ceiling, leads me around shelves of books and down halls to the library's North Carolina Collection. The blue light defines my path to the Hakluyt like a yellow brick road through Oz leads to the Emerald City. It is just one of the many whimsical pieces of art staged in and around this library.

Upstairs in Special Collections, I receive my *Hakluyt*, and with it a pair of white gloves, a magnifying lens, and two blocks of foam to support the binding. I open the book slowly. Something about handling rare books always seduces me: the tobacco smell of leather 400 years old; the laid lines in the yellowed paper; the cache of turnpage words at the bottom of recto pages; the almost illegible gothic type—*almost* the same language I know. People touched this page before me, hundreds of years ago. I open the map of the world. On the east coast of North America, Florida runs slam into Newfoundland, a dent probably indicating the Chesapeake Bay about halfway in-between. Here are English voyages to Africa and Russia and India. Eight hundred pages of voyages, letters about voyages, and patents for exploration. Some are in Latin.

I turn to Hariot's account of the 1587 colony. Here is his mention of the birth: "and because this child was the first Christian borne in Virginia, she was named Virginia."[6] I squint over type so dense with downstrokes it seems a quill may have penned it. Perhaps because of the difficult font, I read more closely. Here is the story of John White's decision to return to England. Several men are pressed to go, agree, sleep on it, and change their minds. What was so urgent? Hariot does not say. Then the colonists as a group beg John White to go. He angrily refuses—twice—giving all kinds of reasonable excuses. It would seem strange for him to leave so soon, leaving everyone behind, after persuading all these colonists to come; people would say he abandoned them. The third time, Hariot reports, the women join in. It is the women who convince him. Would Eleanor have been among them? My eyes are getting tired, the type is so tiny and furry and black. I have to read it again. Surely any father would consider the fate of his daughter and granddaughter in making such a decision.

Hariot does not report his colleague White's thoughts on that. He says White goes because he is convinced that he will be more effective at getting help than anyone else. The colonists write a signed document promising to protect his papers and letting it be known to "you, Your Majesties subjects in England," that White returned at their behest. White goes; he will return, but never stay. He is the most lost of all the colonists.

SUNSET. I walk out of the Joyner Library and into Sonic Plaza. Roman columns chime as I walk past, a single eerie note—more playful art. I find my car, having memorized its location in a lot behind a grove of trees, as if I were some explorer of a trackless wilderness instead of a visitor to a very well-tracked campus. I am notoriously bad at directions. I prefer a landscape with a single road or river going due north, a line I can gauge my progress by. Sometimes I can intuit how a town is laid out in a single glance, but it has to be predictable in some way, follow a pattern that my mind can easily comprehend. This does not describe my experience of Greenville.

I have reservations at the Motel 6, made at 6 o'clock this morning. I think the desk clerk said the motel was northeast of town, on the main road, across from the new mall: "You can't miss it." I consider, briefly, trying to find the site of Sallie Cotten's old plantation. Shields told me that the house has burned down, but that there is a historic marker. It's getting dark, though, and I can't find a road sign. No left turn here, so I take a right and go on faith.

I spend the next twenty minutes traveling out of town in a northeasterly direction. First, over the Tar River on a two-lane camelback bridge, then into some kind of warehouse district. No gas stations, no houses, no road signs. I don't want to turn around because I am convinced I will get a flat tire from all the shards of glass by the side of the road. The light has grown dusky; the road seems deserted. This is the time of day, and the kind of place, where I run slam up against my city paranoia: *Get away from this mess, find a map, find a gas station—preferably one of those big spanking shiny ones with a clean bathroom and strong coffee.* No such luck.

The buildings at the side of the road seem horribly spooky in the twilight. I am surrounded by looming storage tanks and grain elevators, some of them leaning and rickety, some with roofs caved in, some actually crushed, with trash piled up and scattered around them. It looks like a wasteland. Where in the world am I? I have no map. More piles of trash, bagged garbage, rows of rubble, a soggy roll of pink insulation. Then I remember: this area was completely flooded by Hurricane Floyd a month ago. This is the ruin that is left.

On the way here this morning I noticed the roadside grasses and ditches seemed brown and dead, perhaps drowned in toxic waters of the recent disaster. I eyed the gas station attendants, the servers of coffee at McDonald's, wondering about their ruined homes, their flooded lives. Now I wonder again about the people here—were they wiped out? Are their families okay? Are they glad to be alive, with all they lost?

I am still looking for someplace to ask directions. It's getting darker. Between the bare trunks of trees to my left I keep glimpsing car lights and a big highway—surely these two roads will intersect? They do not. There's a light up ahead—a gas station? Anything that's lit up around a place like this has to be a gas station. I squint in the darkness. BAIL BONDSMAN, the sign says. I laugh. Oh no! It might as well say, "THIS NEIGHBORHOOD POPULATED BY FELONS." I keep going.

Finally there's a gas station, one so old it's practically an antique. It has two small pumps, a gravel drive, and no place to park. The tiny bungalow behind the pumps is festooned with Christmas lights. Fake snow frosts the windows, and a neon sign promises HOT DOGS. I wedge my car in between two others pulled into the ditch at a rakish angle. I scope the place out quickly on my woman-traveling-alone-after-dark radar: two guys; nobody drinking or fighting; a couple of motorcycles. A black lady in a Buick Skylark with peeling paint, talking to her friend. A neighborhood place. *Friendly to those it knows.* One fellow gives me a look—I'm out of place here, in my scholar-goes-visiting clothes. I walk inside and wait my turn, the endless country version of "Little Drummer Boy" thrumming in the background.

I smile at the blonde behind the counter: "I don't know where I am," I say ruefully, hoping she'll laugh. The Buick lady turns to me, astonished, and says, "You're in *Greenville*, honey."

After some discussion about a Red Lobster and the New Mall, I follow her Buick to the road I should have been on, the road that was glimmering through the trees in the sunset glare. She turns off to her church's Friday night service. If there were a psalm of gratitude in the *Book of Common Prayer* for finding the right road, I would recite it now. *You're in Greenville, honey*, I whisper, heading back to the lighted path.

Chapter 8:

What's in a Name?

There is a tradition among these people at the present time that their ancestors were the lost colony, amalgamated with some tribe of Indians...
— Special Indian Agent O. M. McPherson,
quoted in *The Only Land I Know: A History of the Lumbee Indians*

[T]he thread of evidence of a connection between these Indians and the Lost Colony is so slender that it will not hold together.
— Douglas L. Rights,
The American Indian in North Carolina

BLUE MEADOW FARM. The story of Virginia Dare collides with modern history in the land of the Lumbee. There, in the coastal flatlands and swamps of the Carolina low country, some say, descendants of Virginia and her English cohorts hid away from their enemies for generations, leaving a legacy of Elizabethan expressions, blue eyes, and family stories.

In my seventeen years in North Carolina, I have acquired a sense of the stories that circulate, true or not, about the Lumbee of Robeson County. What I know about them is more a jumble of memory and apprehension than a set of reliable facts. There are more than 40,000 Lumbee, but they have no reservation and have never been recognized as an independent nation. There is Eddie Hatcher, the Indian activist who took hostages in the eighties to bring local corruption to light. Acquitted of federal charges, he went to jail anyway after a local judge convicted him on state charges. I heard he got out early but had contracted AIDS while in prison.

I've heard stories, too, about Robeson County: of police corruption, cocaine dealing, and profiteering among local white families along the notorious I-95 "Drug Corridor." A few years back, Michael Jordan's father was shot and killed by the side of the road as he slept in his car, near Lumberton. Was it in Robeson County? Probably. Somewhere south of here, in a dimly understood corner of the state, is a place that holds equal populations of black, white, and Indian peoples, a place so racially divided that there have been as many as five separate school systems within a single county. Then there is the notorious local prosecutor, Joe Freeman Britt. He's listed in the *Guinness Book of World Records* as "the world's deadliest district attorney," with forty-six death penalties notched on his belt. Add to the mix stories about the Klan.

In my reading, I learn that some of what I've heard is true. In the recent words of a *Charlotte Observer* reporter, Robeson is "still flat and swampy, still neither a rich place nor a pretty one."

"Even today," the reporter continues, "you're more likely to be murdered and robbed, more likely to drop out of school and lose your job, more likely to get fat and die young [here] than most anywhere else in North Carolina."[1]

Unlike the sleepy waterways north and west of Albemarle Sound, unlike the tourist Mecca of the Outer Banks, this place and people are embroiled in a current historical drama that flares to flame with the heat of past history. History here is alive and kicking and a little terrifying. If I am going to continue my search among the Lumbee, I am going to have to watch my step. I am going to have to study up and at least attempt to get a fuller understanding of how the present fits with the past here. Before I set foot on Lumbee ground, I am going to have to get an inkling of understanding of what happened there for the last 400 years.

As I BEGIN MY READING, I become aware that my probing into the story of the Lumbee people follows a pattern that has gone on before: Outsiders come, poke around, bring up Virginia Dare like some kind of talisman of good will, then leave, with their insights incomplete at best. Yet I am determined to try. Lumbee history is much more than a romantic vision of connection to a blue-eyed daughter of the English. Lumbee history is one of the answers to the question, "What happened to the Indian nations of the Carolinas?"

One of the best places to look for answers to that question, I know, is the journals of John Lawson, the English explorer. Lawson visited the Carolinas in 1701, more than a hundred years after the fates of the Roanoke colonists were sealed, long after the last efforts for finding them were given up. But he came at a pivotal time in the history of Native Americans of the Carolinas. And he made a record of that history that is so thorough and detailed that it is a benchmark for most later study.

On his "journey of a thousand miles" through the heart of North and South Carolina, Lawson recorded twenty or more nations of Native Americans. One, of course, was the Hatteras or "Croatoan" people, among whom he found gray-eyed Indians and stories about Roanoke colony survivors.[2] By the time Lawson arrived, however, some Indian nations had already disappeared.

Lawson's journal records their heartbreaking tales: whole tribes wiped out by slave traders, smallpox, and rum. Of the more than twenty nations listed in Lawson's journal, none were called the Lumbee. Meticulous as he was, could Lawson have missed a significant group such as this? Or were the Lumbee called by another name in his time?

Lawson was so impressed by the many diverse peoples he encountered—and so concerned for their fate—that he made a proposal to his fellow English settlers for ways they could live in peace with the natives: Marry them, convert them, teach them English, and teach them a trade. His theory about the Roanoke colonists was that they must have survived by intermarrying with the Croatoan.

For all his sympathetic feeling for the Native peoples of the Carolinas, Lawson was just another Englishman contributing to their demise. His torture and death at the hands of the Tuscarora in 1711 kicked off a war with the English that laid waste to every intact tribe in the Carolinas but the Cherokee in the far western mountains.

Most tribal people who survived evacuated north and west, joining with stronger groups. When settlers came inland to the Piedmont, they found the land strangely deserted. Lawson might be as surprised as I was to learn that a whole nation survived to the twenty-first century in Eastern Carolina—40,000 or more—by learning English, converting to Christianity, marrying outside their culture, learning trades—and hiding in the swamps of Robeson County.

ALBEMARLE SOUND, 1713. Ellie, grand-daughter to Virginia by five generations, is getting old. The smoke from the common fire now tires her eyes; her hands ache with the cold weather. Ellie leans on a staff of hickory wood to walk, and sometimes she needs the help of her grandson, Wassador. The boy was named for his great value, and his bright color, like the copper ornaments the chief wears. Unlike the chief, however, the boy has gray eyes like hers.

Ellie sees the chief planning their long journey.

She practices walking.

Just as her People once hid in the deep woods and swamps to the north, in her ancestors' time, now they will move again, away from the sickness that has struck so many other villages; away from the warring English; away from the warriors red with paint that crowd the trails.

Her People have kept hidden from the English until the recent Wars. The English steal the children and sell them. Some people say they roast and eat them, but she does not believe that. She has seen these English and they are not demons. They are people, of a sort. Their women love their children. No mother allows such things. Besides, her ancestors were English.

But now so many warring braves have traveled her people's secret paths, burning crops, stealing women; now so many English warriors, with their pale eyes and fine clothes and funny booted stride, have passed so close by. They took her daughter, Wassador's mother. They will keep coming. It will not be long until the leaves drop even from the tangle of grapevine in this deep thicket and reveal the best hiding place of the People.

Traders bring sharps for spears, bird points, and scrapers from a place far south of here, a place that only few know how to find. It is a place, they say, where there are still miles and miles of secret paths; where one wrong step puts the foot in sucking sand that pulls you down. Last month her People sent their fattest corn and their last peach loaf, their tastiest dried fish. They will be welcome there. The People will leave before frost shivers the trees.

Ellie will walk, Wassador beside her. There will be no stopping to rest. The people will fast; the children will eat dried venison from bags they carry at their waists. She will carry little—a pouch of dried berries, peach seeds for planting. She has long since learned that the tiny knot of sweet-sour dried cherry under her tongue keeps the mouth from getting dry on long walks, keeps the mind alert, and the shrunken stomach soft and hopeful.

She will strap to Wassador's strong back a bundle of clean bones wrapped in skins—Virginia's bones. She will bring with her the story of her mother, and her grandmothers before that, and her secret store of English words. These she has kept as a kind of passport of last resort. She keeps the list of names in memory, teaches them to Wassador: Darr, Sampson, Berry, Jones; John White, Raw-leigh, Liz-a-beth; Virginia, Ananias, Eleanor. Sometimes they sound like bird calls from a strange country. When she thinks of her English ancestors, the list of names she keeps in memory, she sometimes feels a secret wealth. Then she looks at all that has been given her by her People, and all that has been taken away by the English, and she is ashamed.

She will save her People if she can, by speaking English words, more powerful than any shaman's spell for sickness.

———

Two twentieth-century Lumbee scholars have produced some of the most convincing arguments that Virginia Dare's people survived among their own; a handful of nineteenth-century white scholars spoke to the connection as well. Lumbee Lew Barton published a history of his people in 1967 entitled *The Most Ironic Story in American History.*[3] He makes his case for Lumbee descent from the Lost Colony, along with newspaper articles, autobiography, and his own poetry. In 1996, Lumbee scholar Dr. Adolph Dial provided one of the more comprehensive reviews of the Roanoke connection in his history of the Lumbee, *The Only Land I Know.*[4] Believing that his own name, "Dial," pronounced "Dal," was a derivative of "Dare," the scholar had a personal interest in unearthing the story. Dial wrote that in 1660, seventy-three years after Virginia Dare was born, a certain Reverend Morgan Jones traveled from Port Royal, South Carolina, northward and was captured by a group of Indians who spoke English. Dial concludes that Jones must have passed through the area now known as Robeson County.

But there is more.

In 1670, John Lederer, a German explorer, traveled south from Virginia into North Carolina and passed through the Robeson County area on his way to South Carolina. He visited a series of tribal people, including the Chowanoc, Tuscarora, Cheraw, and Santee. Near the border of South Carolina, he learned from several Indian traders that "two days' journey and a half from hence to the southwest, a powerful nation of bearded men were seated . . ."[5] Lederer concludes they must be Spaniards, as the Indians themselves do not grow beards. It's true that Spanish explorer Hernando DeSoto had been in Cheraw territory back in 1540, possibly near the border of what is now North and South Carolina.[6] Dial, however, hypothesizes that they could have been Englishmen, either from a colony then settled on the Lower Cape Fear, or from Roanoke. He concludes that all these reports and legends, in conjunction with traditions, family names, and language quirks, amount to firm evidence of Lost Colony survival among the Lumbee—at least for a time.

According to nineteenth-century historian Stephen B. Weeks, there was another account of what could be Croatan Indians mixed with Roanoke survivors. In 1704, traveling as a missionary through settlements at Albemarle Sound, Rev. John F. Blair reported a tribe living to the south, "no less than 100,000, many of which live amongst the English." Weeks concludes Blair's figures are exaggerated, and his descriptions vague, but that the location would indicate Croatan people.[7]

Although scattered English colonies and explorations skirted the area of Robeson County during the 1600s, very little was reported about the interior. Lumbee tradition holds that their ancestors moved from their village along the coast to the Black River, and "it seems likely that they were settled in Robeson County as early as 1650."[8] Into these swamps, people came bearing family names of Chevin, Jones, Berry, and Sampson, names still found among the Lumbee in the late nineteenth century. One of the family names was—according to some—Dare.

Stephen Weeks' source of information was Scot and French Huguenot settlers' descendants. "The universal tradition among the descendants of these settlers," he wrote, "is that their ancestors found a large tribe of Indians located on Lumber river in Robeson County, who were tilling the soil, owning slaves, and speaking English. The descendants of this tribe are known to be the Croatan Indians to-day."[9]

If the descendants of the colony and the remnants of the Hatteras tribe did move inland to these swamps, it was almost two hundred years between the time early explorers made their claims and the time historians began to attempt to put the story together. Much water had passed under the bridge, many seasons of drought and flood, feast and poverty, isolation and interdependence had passed for the survivors in these swamps.

THE CONNECTION BETWEEN ENGLISH PEOPLE AND LUMBEE is a repeated pattern. According to tradition, Lumbee ancestors fought on the English side in the Tuscarora War. Some English troops, returning home from that war, traveled through the blackwater swamps of what is now Robeson County, found clusters of settlers there, and joined them. They had found what was to become known in the nineteenth century as The Settlement, a loose confederation of dwellings over a large area of remote swamp, home to refugees of all stripes. Two things kept Indian people safe and hidden in The Settlement—impenetrable swamps and the even better camouflage of the English language.

Lumbee ancestors gained royal grants of land in the Robeson area as far back as the 1730s. By 1754 there were fifty Indian families living on Drowning Creek without official deeds to the land.[10] Lumbee apparently fought with honor in the Revolutionary War. The Lumbees' independent ways, their remote location, and their lack of an official tribal identity combined with their adoption of English language and culture to keep them safe from extermination into the nineteenth century.

In the 1830s, Andrew Jackson's Indian Removal Act resulted in the forced exile of all tribes east of the Mississippi, even the powerful Cherokee. But the Lumbee, with their English-speaking ways and remote settlements, were again exempt. In 1835, however, when North Carolina's legislature suddenly removed the rights of "free people of color," the Lumbee got caught in a crossfire. The atmosphere of live and let live in the swamps irrevocably changed. Lumbee people became subject to legal and economic harassment by whites eager to grab their lands and property. A cruel new practice of planting "stolen" goods on Lumbee homesteads made it impossible to avoid trouble. The law against Lumbee people owning firearms made it impossible to fight back.

Unlike the "people of color" who were African American slaves, Lowries and Locklears did not consider moving North to freedom, and to go west to reservations never would have occurred to them. They held their ground, slipping into the mist when they could evade conflict, and fighting when they could not. It took the Civil War to light a fuse that would explode the idea of hiding away in the swamps. That firestorm also brought to light the questions about the Lumbee connection to the Lost Colony. During the Civil War, the Lumbee's greatest folk hero emerged: Henry Berry Lowrie.

The story of outlaw Henry Berry Lowrie is one of the most powerful Lumbee legends, this one firmly based in history. It too has a Lost Colony connection. Some say the "Henry Berry" in Lowrie's name could be traced back to the ship's roster at Roanoke. During the war, the Home Guard and local conscriptors drafted Lumbee men and boys into slavery to dig earthworks at Fort Fisher. Lowrie hid away in the swamps with a band of Lumbee, black, and Scot outlaws to avoid the brutal treatment. They stole food from those who had it and distributed to those who needed it. Treated badly by their white neighbors, especially conscription officer Brant Harris, Lumbee began to favor the Union side, and their tradition of taking in refugees now included Union soldiers.

The plot thickened when Brant Harris shot two Lowrie boys returning on leave from the conscription camps. Their stone-eyed father spoke at their funeral, saying, "We have always been friends of white men. We were a free people long before the white men came to our land. Our tribe lived in Roanoke in Virginia...."[11] He continued, giving what seemed to be a brief but complete history of family connection to the Roanoke colony. This account would be recorded, word for word, by local historian Hamilton McMillan, and would be at the center of his later claims of the Lumbee's common history with the colonists.

When his father and brother were set up by the Home Guard and shot in cold blood, Henry Berry Lowrie vowed revenge. He and his gang shot the conscription master, the sheriff, and Brant Harris. In an effort to force Lowrie to surrender, his wife, Rhoda, and other outlaw wives were captured and held at the jail. But Lowrie's gang signed a letter—

reportedly "in their own blood"—demanding their return and threatening a bone-chilling revenge on the women and children of the captors. Such was Lowrie's reputation that Rhoda was set free, no questions asked.

"The Lowrie War" continued well into Reconstruction, until the last of the gang was shot by bounty hunters. Henry Berry Lowrie was reported dead, but no body was ever brought to light, despite a handsome reward. They say his fierce spirit still haunts the Lumbee people. Today, an annual award is given in his name to "the citizen who best exemplifies the highest standard of service to the community."[12] But during Lowrie's time, the feud bred a toxic new racism that would set neighbor against neighbor in a place that had been known as a safe harbor for lost people of every kind.

IN THE HUNDRED OR MORE YEARS SINCE Henry Berry Lowrie died, a new Lumbee struggle has emerged: The fight for recognition as an Indian nation. In this struggle, too, the mystery of Lost Colony survivors plays a role. It was not the Lumbee but Scotsman Hamilton McMillan who made the first move for tribal recognition in a pamphlet he published called *Sir Walter Raleigh's Lost Colony: A Historical Sketch of the Attempts of Sir Walter Raleigh to Establish a Colony in Virginia, with the Traditions of an Indian Tribe in North Carolina, Indicating the Fate of the Colony of Englishmen Left on Roanoke Island in 1587.*

As a state legislator and historian from Robeson, McMillan convinced the North Carolina General Assembly to recognize the mysterious tribe of Robeson County as "Croatan Indians," apparently assuming that John White had got the name right in the first place. McMillan gave proof in the journals of Lawson and Lederer, and in the survival of forty-one out of ninety-five Roanoke surnames among the Indians. Although today's most common Lumbee surnames Locklear and Oxendine, Brayboy and Lowrie, are not on John White's roster, there were Berrys, Sampsons, Joneses, and others.

Called, variously, "the best white friend the Lumbee ever had" and "a politician looking for votes," McMillan was no doubt a little of both. To his credit, he won quite a coup for his time, almost a thousand dollars to pay for teachers and construction for a Croatan Normal School.

Historian Stephen B. Weeks's treatise followed in 1891, in which he argued that the "habits, disposition, and mental characteristics" of the "Croatan" Indians showed English ancestry, along with the family name connections and the Elizabethan flavor to their English language. He reported that the Croatan "believe themselves to be the descendants of the colonists of 1587, and boast of their mixed English and Indian blood." Weeks notes the Indian habit of referring to eastern Carolina as "Virginia" (Carolina was Virginia in the colonists' time), and says old-timers recall the story of Virginia Dare, "but her name is preserved only as Darr, Durr, Dorr." Weeks also lists colonists' surnames and notes the similarities McMillan found. These names, he reports, "now rarely met with in North Carolina, are reproduced by a tribe living hundreds of miles from Roanoke Island, and after a lapse of three hundred years."[13]

The South I live in still holds on to the tradition of getting to know you by asking about your people. Instead of "What do you do?," people ask, "Who's your daddy?" and "Where's your homeplace?" Sometimes a name gives a connection. Sometimes a church or a road. In Chatham County, I'm a Hudson—but, I explain, not a Chatham County Hudson: "My husband's people are from Dunn." Then, if the conversation lags, I can say, "My husband's a Morris on his mother's side. Did you know his grandfather?" I'm sure Lumbee people answer the question "Who are your people?" without difficulty. But the outside world has had one heck of a time placing them in a category. It certainly has tried.

Sometime before January 7, 1889, the "honorable Congress of the United States" received a petition from fifty-four Locklears, Oxendines, Sampsons, Lowries and others, asking for funding to educate their children in order to "fit them for the duties of American citizenship."[14] The Office of Indian Affairs had no idea who these people were. Commissioner Oberly wrote, "I can find no reference to them in any history at my command," and asked for help from the Smithsonian Institution's Bureau of Ethnology.[15] The Bureau referred him to Hamilton McMillan. McMillan responded with a history of the Croatan tribe, giving his full argument for the Roanoke connection.

A Mr. W. L. Moore, from Robeson, followed up the plea for federal education funding in a series of letters. The response was short. Although expressing deep regret that state funding was inadequate, and showing great interest in the history of the tribe, T. J. Morgan, Commissioner of

Indian Affairs, wrote Moore to say there simply wasn't enough money to educate the 36,000 Indian children already under protection of the U.S. Government. How could they take on more?

Oddly, the adoption of the English language and culture in this tribe that had ensured their survival would also eventually frustrate "Croatan" bids for official recognition. Unsuccessful proposals to benefit the Lumbee by naming them continued to dog the tribe. Some simply backfired. By 1911, the "Croatan" label adopted earlier had become a derogatory term, so the state's General Assembly passed a resolution to name them "Indians of Robeson County." In 1914, another Scot, lawyer Angus Wilton McLean, convinced the local legislature of Lumbee descent from the Cherokee and from the Lost Colonists. So, for a time the Indians of Robeson were known as "Cherokee Indians of Robeson County."

In 1934 a group petitioned Congress to change the name to "Siouan Indians of the Lumber River." That petition failed. Finally, in 1953, the Indians themselves voted to call themselves the Lumbee, after the river that meanders through the Robeson lowlands. The state legislature passed the law, followed by the U.S. Congress in 1956. It would be the first time Lumbee people had chosen their own "official" identity, unaided by enthusiastic white scholars.

In 1958, on a dark January night, the Lumbee people took hold of their destiny in a new way: they attended a Ku Klux Klan rally, took it over, and ran the surprised troublemakers into the swamps. A Lumbee judge convicted several Klansmen and sent them to jail. A tide had turned.

After years of name changes and confusion, the Lumbee name stuck. Through the next few decades, Lumbee people made gains in education and economic development. Various forms of tribal government emerged. Pembroke College expanded and became part of the University of North Carolina system. The Lumbee still hope for full federal recognition of the tribe. But their petitions have not had much luck.

Since a new federal law governing Native American tribal recognition was passed in 1978, seventy-two groups have actually submitted petitions, including the Lumbee. Only fifteen petitions resulted in actual federal recognition. The petition process contained a kind of Catch-22 for the Lumbee. When Congress acknowledged them in 1956, the legislation limited federal funding of the group. The petition process could not proceed without an amendment or change to that law. The Lumbee petition was turned down. In a somewhat ominous note, the Bureau website says, "Only one BIA decision in the past twenty years has been overturned by a Federal court." [16]

The tribe turned to the legislative process.

In 1988 North Carolina's Representative Charlie Rose introduced a bill that would amend the previous law and allow full recognition. The Lumbee were the largest Indian group east of the Mississippi, and the ninth largest in the country. Recognizing that full federal funding for more than 40,000 Lumbee Indians could threaten budget allotments for other tribes, the legislation stipulated that the tribe would seek funding outside of the existing BIA budget.

Cynthia Hunt at Lumbee River Legal Services explains, "We bent over backwards in this process to keep from diminishing benefits to other tribes." She adds that the Lumbee did not seek all federal benefits available, just those that would support health care, housing, and education. The bill passed the full House and made it to the floor of the Senate, only to be voted down by two votes. One of the votes was North Carolina's own Senator Jesse Helms, known as "Senator No" for his habit of opposing progressive legislation.

In order to be fully recognized by the U.S. government, the Lumbee must pass muster on seven points: they must be able to prove Indian identity since 1900; they must have functioned as a distinct community; they must have political autonomy and a unified tribal leadership; they must have a tribal governing document; they must not claim to be members of another tribe; and their identity must not have been denied in previous laws. A recent court case has resolved conflicts over tribal leadership, and work is under way to create governing documents.

Indian cultural identity is often defined by such things as religion, traditional stories, ritual, and language. When they adopted English culture, the Lumbee long ago lost connection to Native religious beliefs and rituals. Having adopted the English language, they claim no traditional Siouan, Algonkian, or Iroquoian tongue. Their way of speaking, however, has long intrigued outsiders.

In 1998, sociolinguistic scholar Dr. Walt Wolfram of North Carolina State University released a study about the unique Lumbee dialect. The study reviewed Adolph Dial's oral histories and conducted another 150 interviews with Lumbee people. Although the Lumbee have been speaking English for 200 years, he reported, their speech differs from that of other regional English speakers in some significant ways. He was surprised to find "examples of linguistic affinity" with the dialect of the Outer Banks, said to contain remnant Elizabethan expressions and pronunciation. But the isolated similarities were not enough, he concluded, to confirm any link to Lost Colony survivors. Rather, they simply confirm a unique language heritage among Lumbee people.[17] A video documentary released in the year 2000 concludes that one of the ways Lumbee know their own is by words and expressions found nowhere else.[18] In telling their own story, the Lumbee people use their own words, quite literally.

New linguistic studies have helped define the unique culture of the Lumbee. When the political climate is right, the next attempt for recognition may succeed.

These days, claims of descent from English colonists is much beside the point, and even counterproductive. From time to time on my journey, people have asked me why folks don't get DNA tests to prove descent from Virginia Dare. Nobody has done it that I know of—for one thing, there is no DNA sample to match. I can't imagine that any Lumbee people would want to define themselves by her—who they are is a unique people with links to many cultures.

As one of the Lumbee's active advocates for recognition, Cynthia Hunt says, "I truly don't believe we are descended from the Lost Colony. There is blonde hair and blue eyes in Lumbee people for generations— but there were English traders coming among us for centuries." She doesn't buy the story about similar surnames, either, nor family stories of connections to "Roanoke."

"McMillan heard elders talking," she says, "about coming from Roanoke in Virginia—but it was the *other* Roanoke in Virginia they meant—the Roanoke River." Hunt says Dr. Dial was a great believer in the Lost Colony theory, however, and that she knows folks alive today who truly believe they are descended from Virginia Dare's people. "My grandmother," she muses, "died thinking she was a Croatan."

THE RIDDLE OF THE LUMBEE PEOPLE will not be solved by reading more about them. Perhaps the scholars at UNC-Pembroke can help. My search points toward the largest concentration of Native Americans on the East Coast—and the most mysterious—the Lumbee of Robeson County.

Chapter 9:

The Road to Robeson

The inhabitants are natives and have lived there forever.
I am the only stranger.
> —Richard Hugo, from
> "Assumptions," in *The Triggering Town*

ROUTE 87. DECEMBER 7, 2000. The road to Robeson County cuts through piedmont North Carolina across the Cape Fear watershed and into the drainage of the Lumber River on the coastal plain. Watery fingers spread southward across the land, joining the blackwater river: Burnt Swamp, Bear Swamp, Jordan Swamp, Saddletree. The river shrugs east and west, defining a dark rippled thread across drained land and pocosin, confining itself inside twenty-foot banks in drought times, widening its reach into cottonfields in flood. On my North Carolina map, it is called the Lumber River, but locals call it the Lumbee.

If you're not careful once you turn onto I-95, you may miss Lumbee territory altogether, overwhelmed by all the signs for South of the Border near the South Carolina line. I remember early incarnations of these signs from family trips to Florida in the sixties—and from twenty-something joyrides in the seventies to buy cheap cigarettes in Myrtle Beach. "Pedro," a headless cipher in a neon-blazing poncho and enormous hat, urges children to "Yell louder, they'll stop!" Now I regard him with exasperation, wondering what Mexican migrants who work the fields here must think of his obnoxious rant. Nobody stops much in this part of Robeson County, unless it's to gas up and buy a burger and move on. Folks on 95 are mostly headed somewhere else.

I make my exit onto Route 711 toward Pembroke, away from the population center in Lumberton. I have been told I must have a Lumbee guide to this place in order to understand it; I have none. For the first time in my journey I look through the windshield with real trepidation—this place is so isolated and insular, anyone with any sense will know I am a stranger, and strangers might not be as welcome nowadays as they used to be.

It's a feeling I haven't had since I first moved to rural North Carolina, as an urban Yankee with D.C. plates on my car, during a time when the term "Washington" was tantamount to a curse in the South. From all the stories I've heard about Klan rallies and racism and corruption, white strangers may be suspect here—and if not suspect, then at least tiresome and nosy. Searching for Virginia Dare will make it hard to float unobserved. I will be blindingly, unredeemably, one more white person with something to prove.

Route 711 seems to travel through a place out of time. Flat fields spread a hundred acres on either side and snags of longleaf pine and oak rag the horizon. One low spot in the road sprouts a clump of "mistletoe trees"—bare oak branches pomponned with dark green puffs of foliage. Another branch drifts with Spanish moss. The burnt-soil smell is people firing their ditches, an age-old farm tradition, one that may date back to Native American practices. Today a thin sheet of smoke hovers in the clear air above the fields. A freak snowstorm a week ago has left crusts of white in the shady sides of longleaf pines. Shreds of cotton fiber left behind at harvest straggle across unplowed fields like a the weave of a threadbare sweater. One plowed field advertises "New Homes, Lots." A crossroads features an Indian Trading Post, colorful with painted designs.

The town of Pembroke is about ten miles from I-95, but a world apart. Here is the center of culture and activity for a tribe of 47,000 Lumbee Indians, who live spread out across Robeson and neighboring counties in a loose community. The Lumbee are the "largest Indian tribe in the nation without a reservation," according to a local tourist brochure. Main Street cuts through neighborhoods of small neat houses, some exuberantly decorated for the season. Railroad tracks bisect the town, clacking freights stop traffic at the crossing for long stretches at a time. They don't seem to slow down much. Past the railroad tracks there's a block of shops whose light poles glitter with Christmas decorations. Shimmery loops form slightly misshapen Santas and candles and trees. Everything looks ready for the local Christmas parade. I wonder if it's scheduled for this weekend.

The fourth traffic light is the signal for my turn, across more railroad tracks, to the most venerable building on the campus of the University of North Carolina at Pembroke: Old Main. A distinctive arrowhead decoration about the size of a man and a half marks the entrance. To the right is a statue of a man in a suit, caught mid-stride, going somewhere in a hurry: Hamilton McMillan, the Scot who won the first funding for Lumbee education.

Today Old Main is the home of the American Indian Studies Department and the Native American Resource Center. The Department is unique on the East Coast—a place where people can study Hopi and Navaho art, Woodland and Archaic points and tools, American Indian literature—and probably the only place in the world where Lumbee study Lumbee.

Dr. Stanley Knick is director of the Center and curator of its museum. He's such a champion of the local culture that, a local confides, he is a rare Caucasian adoptee into the Lumbee tribe. His manifesto on the Web is one reason I am here. An article he posted called "Because It Is Right" gives archeological evidence of continuous Indian occupation in Robeson—along with an argument for Lumbee federal recognition.

Knick says his approach to anthropology is holistic. "In order to appreciate a culture," he explains, "you must take a very broad view." His work spans much more than digs—it includes oral histories, health studies, accounts of herbal healing, local art exhibits, and just plain listening. His archeological research in 1987-88 created a new baseline for study of Lumbee territory.[1] Using nine U.S. Geological Survey maps, Knick and a team of students and locals visited 316 locations and found archeological sites of interest at 314 of them. The vast majority contained Indian artifacts.

"It was a reconnaissance," Knick says. "The idea was to see how many sites you could find." How did he know where to dig? Knick used what he calls the "intuitive/opportunistic" approach, following leads and thinking about likely locations of human habitation. Earlier studies pointed the way to several sites.

Knick's survey showed that Robeson County has been inhabited by Native Americans for more than 10,000 years. The artifacts found reflect a small population during Paleo-Indian times, a larger one in the Archaic period, still more in the Woodland period. European occupation may be inferred by the presence of kaolin pipe stems—the kind Englishmen used to smoke tobacco. When, exactly, were those Europeans here? Could they have been the Lost Colonists?

"It would be nice to find a 1582 coin of the realm at the same site with Woodland artifacts," Knick jokes. But, he says, he was able to date a group of English pipe artifacts by measuring the diameters of the smoke holes and using an averaging formula. The average date of the pipes found here is 1727 or thereabouts. Some in the collection may have been made twenty to thirty years before that—before the time of colonial land grants, but long after first English contact. It's entirely possible, Knick says, that European trade goods reached this area before Europeans themselves. The "Old Lowry Road" was a major trading route for the Cheraw and other tribes. The Cheraw were important middlemen in trade between the Jamestown colony and the Catawba nation to the west. Nothing conclusive there, but some tempting connections to the Lost Ones.

Before the English came, North Carolina was home to three major Native American culture groups—Algonkian, Iroquoian, and Siouan—each with different languages and traditions. The Lumbee River flowed at the juncture those groups' geographic territories. Scholars seeking Lumbee roots tend to favor the "Cheraw Theory," in combination with several other possibilities that Knick jokingly calls "All of the Above." The Cheraw theory postulates that Lumbee people evolved from Cheraw Indians and related Siouan tribes who occupied the area both before and after European settlement. After European contact began to break up Native patterns of occupation, émigrés from the Iroquoian and Algonkian tribes joined the Siouan people occupying the Lumbee River lowlands. The Hatteras—or Croatoan—Indians may have been among the Algonkian émigrés. They may have brought descendants of the English colonists. English became the common language within the Lumbee River community.

All the threads of heritage fit tightly in this theory, like the weave of a pine needle basket. Lacking detailed documentation from early explorers, many scholars had assumed that the swamps of Robeson had no lengthy history of Indian occupation. Knick's archeology studies belie that assumption.

Knick's Phase I survey team found a Clovis point—"the only documented Clovis-like projectile point in Robeson County"—and a Hardaway point, both indicators of Archaic Indian culture—that is, from the time of earliest known occupation, 14,000 years ago. Follow-up research in 1992 uncovered one undisturbed site that was a mother lode.

Site 31Rb430 is a low hill, thought to be a burial mound. It revealed, in a single 5-foot test unit, an incredible diversity and wealth of pottery sherds and points from Archaic through Late Woodland periods. Knick concludes the site was a longtime Native factory or repair shop for stone tools, with stone materials brought in from remote mines. This find gives strong credence to the argument that Lumbee people have made their home here a long time, and that they are certainly not all from somewhere else. This, of course, is something the Lumbee seem to have known all along.

When I tell Knick about the Kendall ring found on Hatteras—a find that seems almost too good to be true, being linked to an exact name and time, and being glimmeringly gold to boot—he says, "The most important connection we have here to the Lost Colony is oral history. There is not now any archeological record that supports the oral histories. Every other piece of information is completely circumstantial." He says some families still claim a connection to the Lost Colony. Others reject the idea entirely. "I tend to be a believer," Knick says of the connection. "But I sure can't prove it."

Knick keeps transcripts of precious Lumbee oral history interviews conducted by the late Adolph Dial. During the late sixties and seventies Dial interviewed elders—sometimes family members, often people he seemed to know well. As he gently guides folks through the questions, the stories about their lives and old times, Dial returns again and again to this question: Did you ever hear about your family being connected to the Roanoke colonists? Some say yes. Some provide elaboration. All are long since dead.

Lumbee people are true Southerners, with a love of grits and country ham, gospel music and family reunions, but they have traveled far and wide in the twentieth century, establishing their own colonies in Northern cities such as Baltimore and Detroit. What traditions bring this diverse people together, linked as they are to black, white, and Native culture? One of the things that indisputably connects Lumbee people, says Knick, is the river. Its black, smooth waters beckon and soothe. If you tried to put up "no swimming" signs here, people would ignore them. "The river has a magical pull," Knick says. He tells a story about two Lumbees sitting at a bar in Baltimore on a hot summer day. "Wanna go swimming?" one says. The other says, "Yeah, let's go." They get in their car and, with no further discussion, drive 400 miles to the shores of the Lumbee. Its healing waters had called them home.

Pembroke Campus. Thursday afternoon. I find myself looking at the faces around me, wondering who is Lumbee and who isn't. The young woman with the tawny square face and dark eyes—maybe. The cluster of blondes whisking down the sidewalk, giddy after exams—maybe not. Two African-Americans studying in the library—who knows?

What is the evidence of being Lumbee? The eye scans for evidence of a pattern to create meaning. I become quickly, embarrassingly, aware of race differences and hidden features—dark versus blue eyes, a certain slant to a cheekbone, a square jaw, an umber cast to skin—all perfect stereotypes, I'm sure, based on my ignorance. The more I look the more uncertain of my own judgments I become. With my flyaway dark-and-silver hair, and my serious brown eyes, I wonder if I could pass. To an outsider like me, it seems almost anybody could. I hear, though, that even with their rainbow of features, the Lumbee always know their own.

I remember an acquaintance confiding that her blonde-haired, blue-eyed adopted child was Lumbee. The adoption agency insisted the new family erase all reference to the baby's surname in its new life, to safeguard the child from prejudice. If it were possible to trace this child's bloodline back to some member of the Lowrie band, or some survivor of a remnant tribe and a Scot turpentiner—or even all the way back to Virginia Dare and some nephew of Manteo's—it would be a fascinating route, I'm sure.

The more I research my own family history—which I once dismissed as embarrassingly, boringly WASP—the more it seems full of unexplored tangents.

The practice of looking to the past for present status makes my head spin—it's a little arrogant, a little like trying to trace one's blood back to Eve, or believing that in a previous life you were someone rich and famous. If any of us traced our families back 400 years, we don't know what stories we would find, what connections and disconnections. Human beings have an affinity for secrets.

When friends and neighbors learn of my search for Virginia Dare, and my quest to uncover the secrets of the mysterious Lumbee, a surprising number of them make a confession: *I am part Indian.* This happens over and over: Librarians, businessmen, Episcopalians, brothers-in-law of friends. We live in a nation of people connected to the ghosts of past nations—and present ones—some of which have nothing to do with European culture.

The Lumbee come in many shapes and colors, and seeing who is and who isn't, is almost beside the point. Everyone is, who knows she is. If you don't know, you are an outsider.

After a stint at the library I head to my hotel in darkness. Downtown on a Friday night things are getting lively. Outside Pembroke the road narrows and I must pull in front of a pickup truck to change lanes. Highbeams blast my rearview mirror. For the next six miles of dark two-lane, the pickup hugs my tail. I can't decide whether to slow down so he will pass or speed up to get away. Is the truck driver pissed off and drunk, or is he an off-duty cop scoping out a stranger? I keep my foot on the accelerator at precisely fifty-five miles per hour.

ADOLPH DIAL AMPHITHEATER. FRIDAY NOON. The Lumbee have their own outdoor theater—this one with a backdrop of blackwater lake and longleaf pine, with rough bench seats and modest light and sound towers. The drama featured here every summer is *Strike at the Wind*, the story of the Lumbee people and Henry Berry Lowrie. The brochure from the 1993 production says the amphitheater stands near an Indian village dating from 800 BC—and the site of an old Lowrie gang hideout.

Sixteen million pounds of earth was trucked in to shape a hillside for the seating.

It's tempting to compare this place to the tourist attraction at Manteo. *The Lost Colony* is consistently one of the top five attractions among outdoor theaters nationwide, with almost 70,000 attendees in the year 2000. Though its first year brought more than 17,000 playgoers, *Strike* attracted only 3,200 in 1997, the last year for which figures are available. The production attracts mostly local residents, though it is marketed during the summer months to tourist families. I'm about six months early, but I have seen no glossy brochures promoting this play. I have seen some for Paul Green's *Lost Colony* in the tourist racks at my hotel—though I am much closer to Pembroke than to Manteo.

Scott Parker, Director of the Institute of Outdoor Drama in Chapel Hill, says there are two main reasons a locality stages a historical drama— to promote appreciation of its local history and to make money. *The Lost Colony* generates up to $20 million in direct and peripheral revenue for the Manteo area, he says. I'm thinking the Pembroke area would surely appreciate such an infusion of cash.

Strike at the Wind has been produced since 1976 under various directors. Its roster of actors over the years is replete with Locklears, Lowries, and Oxendines. Program mug shots show Caucasian, Native, and African American features throughout—more evidence that Lumbee identity is inclusive. For a time the play's lead role was taken by Pembroke native Melton Lowery, a bearded young man with hooded eyes. Melton is listed as a great-great-great-great-grandson of Henry Berry Lowrie himself, who seems in historical photos to be a moody-looking and dour Scotsman. The resemblance is striking.

I'm told this production at times resembles a small-town reunion, with its own rites and rituals. One attendee reported watching while local audience members recognized the players and applauded their entrances. They laughed at odd places, called out familiar lines, and cheered love and death with equal fervor. It sounds like a local variant of the *Rocky Horror Picture Show*. I would love to see it, but December is decidedly the wrong season. Today the bare theater seats give a view of sparkling cold water; the scent of longleaf pines is more reminiscent of Christmas than of Southern summer nights.

The author of the play, Dr. Randolph Umberger, came to the project in 1970 after studying the Cherokee drama *Unto These Hills*. He considered focusing on the Lost Colony connection to the Lumbee, but concluded it was not dramatically compelling enough. "[O]nly one character was historically viable—Henry Berry Lowrie."[2] Still, the story of the colonists provides context. In the script I've found, the narrator, or "Leader" of the story is a Hatteras chief, whose costume is to be modeled after John White drawings. A Greek chorus of Lumbee give the history of the Lost Colony. A colonist, an armored Elizabethan soldier, and a cross-toting missionary parade across the stage. A female voice says: "The English said their colony was lost—but it wasn't." The chorus claims they helped the English when Powhatan attacked, and took them to the Lumbee River to hide.

A voice interjects: *My eyes are not the color of the sky for nothing.*

Another voice claims: *My great-great-great-great-great grandmother was Virginia Dare.*

Another says the "Lowrey" name was once pronounced "Raleigh."

Others claim their names match those of the ship's roster.[3]

Here, nightly on stage, in the heat of summer, Virginia Dare's name is invoked, her people embodied by actors who may actually be related to her. For certain these actors embody the family stories of the Lumbee.

A romantic lyricism weaves among their lines:

Love is the second discovery of fire...

and

Tonight we celebrate the two realities of man—what was, and what might have been...[4]

The idealism is appealing, almost childlike, in our cantankerous time. "This play was a real outgrowth of the spirit of the sixties," says Dr. Robert Reising, literature professor at UNC-Pembroke and board member of the Robeson Historical Drama Association. He points out that the story focuses on "the fight for civil rights and the opposition to oppression." I have noticed that the scenes show the interplay of the many forms of racial prejudice at work along the Lumbee River during the time of the Civil War. Indians insult black slaves; slaves retort; at least one Confederate white attempts to make peace; other Rebs resent him, revealing he is part Cherokee. Actors "take sides" in the play— black, Lumbee, white—articulating every possible point of view. It is the most honest portrayal of the sad anatomy of prejudice that I can imagine. Bravo, Mr. Umberger.

Strike at the Wind was not the first play about the Lowrie gang. Turns out Paul Green wrote and produced a short play called *The Last of the Lowries*—his first to be produced by Carolina Playmakers, on April 30, 1920. Green based his work on an even earlier play by John Synge, *Riders to the Sea*, and on Mary C. Norment's account in *The Lowrey History*.[5] Dramatizing the last stand of the Lowry gang, *The Last of the Lowries* is told from the women's point of view, and leaves out any mention of Lost Colonists.

The most recent depiction of the Lumbee drama in literature is Josephine Humphreys' novel *Nowhere Else on Earth*, told from the viewpoint of Rhoda Strong, the self-described "Queen of Scuffletown" and the wife of Henry Berry Lowrie. Local scholars say it's a good depiction of Lumbee life in the swamps during the Civil War and Reconstruction. Rhoda's voice makes an occasional move toward lyric description of the land: *"Green came before it was due, running the risk of a late freeze. In the scuppernongs, nubs of green popped out on the trunk of the vine, and fernheads pushed their coiled heads up . . ."*[6]

In Humphreys' tale, the world is a skein of secret trails, hideouts, and pocosin. As raiders and Home Guards rage through the swamps, Rhoda and her family hide in their one-room house. One character, a local doctor and historian, keeps measuring people's heads to see if they are of English blood or Indian. He is in mid-rant about the Lost Colonists when the baby he is delivering interrupts and turns the human drama toward the real and immediate joy of a mother and grandmother. Who cares about those crazy colonists?

Humphreys' story layers Lumbee pride and family loyalty over a legacy of violence and poverty. Such a braid of loss and hardship makes a binding tie. The shared history of life in the swamps lives and sweats and breathes. I begin to see where Virginia Dare stands in the midst of this people's drama. For most Lumbee, she holds little of the blue-eyed fascination that seems to have captured folks elsewhere. The kinds of losses counted in the Lumbee experience are a bit more immediate; the questions of identity are questions of survival. They don't have much to do with a little English child born 400 years ago.

Writer, storyteller, and scholar Barbara Braveboy-Locklear grew up in Robeson County, and she confirms to me how very little Virginia Dare's fate has to do with life here. "She is not an important part of our history," she says, in what must be the understatement of the week. "She's just a footnote." If the colonists came here, she says, they have long since been absorbed. Their distinguishing features—language and religion and names—have dissolved into modern Indian culture. The Lumbee, on the other hand, are not going to go away. "The fact that we have survived hundreds of years of contact with other cultures means we will keep surviving," Braveboy-Locklear says. How about federal recognition, that key to economic survival? "It may not happen in my lifetime, but it will in my grandchildren's." Braveboy-Locklear considers herself an elder, so that time may not be as far off as it sounds.

Braveboy-Locklear is writing a book about three Croatan characters. Is it fiction or history? That remains to be seen. Will it include Virginia Dare? I doubt it.

The place where people make the strongest claims about Virginia Dare is the place where she matters the least. And yet, her very disappearance into history and legend keeps her name alive.

———

JUST DOWN THE WAY FROM OLD MAIN, past the library and the university president's house, is the Indian Education Resources Center, a yellow brick structure with a National Register plaque on the entrance wall:

Federal Works Agency
John M. Carmody
Franklin D. Roosevelt

Built in 1939 as Pembroke Indian High School, this structure now acts as museum, art gallery, learning lab, and research center, with Lumbee Bruce Barton acting as curator and director. Barton's father was Lew

Barton, author of *The Most Ironic Story in American History*. In his book Lew Barton lists twenty "known facts" about the Lumbee, including this eye-opening assertion: "They are one of the very few groups of people of American Indian ancestry to retain possession of their original lands."[7] An astonishing accomplishment—and ironic indeed. Lacking official treaties of any kind with the U.S. government turned out to be a stroke of luck. Lumbees were able to keep their land by simply adopting the English practice of holding title to it.

Inside the museum, displays of artifacts, stuffed birds and animals, clothing, tools, and documents crowd the walls and cases. Barton leads me to the VCR and sets me up with three recent videos about the Lumbee people. One of them begins, "To be born a Lumbee Indian is to be born singing. . . ."[8] Three women harmonize a hymn over sizzling frycakes. The beauty of their voices makes me want to go to church. The camera moves into the lap of a family gathering. What makes up Lumbee culture? This film, made by a Lumbee student at UNC-Chapel Hill, opens up the mystery. The Lumbee story is a family story.

The more I watch the filmmaker's depiction of family life, the more her voice reflects the personal, insulated intimacy of her own family, the more I understand what it means, and the more I feel left out. Even the quirky language—filled with special words like "ellick" (sweet cup of coffee) and "mommuck" (to make a mess of something)—is like a secret code for intimacy. Happy families are all alike, Tolstoy said. I know the Lumbee have their share of family trouble. But for the moment, it seems my search has left me looking through a lighted window from the outside. It is a familiar location.

Bruce Barton shows off the contemporary Lumbee art on display in his gallery. He talks a little bit about his travels around Europe as a young man and admits, when prodded, to writing poetry. His father wrote passionately about the Lumbee connection to the Colony, as if it were part and parcel of his personal mission of Lumbee educational opportunity. I want to ask Barton what it's like for him to be carrying on his father's work. Instead, I ask him what he thinks became of Virginia Dare. "I think if she survived, she got married and had twelve or fourteen kids and died in childbirth." Barton does not claim a family connection—or if he does, he is not telling.

Barton turns to converse with an old friend who is visiting—another outsider, but one who lived here for a time. I overhear them make plans to meet for breakfast. The museum is closing, it's time to go, and I leave with a sense of disconnection that is palpable. I do what I always have done when I feel this way—I get in my car and drive.

DRIVING THE BACK ROADS, watching the sunset blaze across the flatlands, I am aware more than ever that the Lumbee community excludes me— whether by intent or circumstance, it does not matter. It may be completely in my own mind. Something Bruce Barton said about his youthful travels undams a flood of memory.

In 1972, shortly after I graduated high school, I left home on a Greyhound bus going west—as far as Ohio. I didn't think so at the time, but I was following the pattern of my ancestors who went West to the frontier in the 1850s, which in those days was somewhere near St. Louis. I was just thinking "Midwest," which was where I was born, and "escape," which was my mantra for many years whenever there was trouble. My family had the usual troubles of families in the crazy seventies, with some dramatic and painful extremes. I had the usual methods of escape.

In the last year of high school I spent most of my time skipping school, cruising way out in the country to pick weeds, get stoned, and skinny dip with my friends. I myself never took my clothes off, being terribly shy.

That moment of departure in the bus station confirmed what I had been practicing most of my senior year: I loved the romance of leaving, not knowing where you're bound. "Lord, I'm 500 miles away from home," I lipped to the smudgy bus window, frosting the glass with my breath— exaggerating, as usual. I wrote an ode to the strip malls we passed on the way out of town, the kind of disdainful poem an eighteen-year-old writes when she plans never to return to her tired old hometown. My obsessive reading of Jack London and Hemingway stories in my youth now dimly informed my launch into the world. I was not going to Alaska, of course, or Spain—only Ohio. But it was far from home and anything could happen.

In the next few years I learned to hitchhike cross-country, sometimes with friends, sometimes alone, making solo pilgrimages out into the dangerous world of guys driving cars. Once, I got into a van full of what looked like friendly hippies. I realized a few miles down the road that the shadowy heap at the back of the vehicle was a pile of carcasses—possum, squirrel, raccoon—and that the guns that shot them were lying back there too—fully loaded, for all I knew.

In one of my proudest feats of denial, I decided that if I didn't show my fear, these killers of small defenseless animals would have to be nice guys. I told them my troubles. Told them I was looking for old friends, didn't know how to get there. Told them I was hungry. I opened my heart to them, as if to say, *Shoot me now, or become someone kind.* They surprised me. They became kind. They bought me a drive-through French fries. They figured out the roads. They drove me to my door, a town at least forty miles out of their way.

Over the next ten years, I counted the places I lived. At one point, there were twenty. I house-sat for strangers, crashed with people I barely knew, slept in attic rooms for rents under fifty dollars. I spent some winter months on an abandoned farm near the West Virginia border, fixing up an old barn in exchange for Food Stamp tuna fish and whole-wheat macaroni and a wood stove that threw out a little heat. One summer I shared a room in a house near the river known as "The Gritty," a place where we deemed cockroaches "Foggy Bottom Water Bugs" in order to joke them out of our hair and food.

One winter I camped on the unheated porch of a house popularly known as "Kensington Dump House" because—as a friend of ours liked to say—"It's a dump, and it's practically all the goddamn way to Kensington." Once my father helped me drag my laundry up to the front door. There was a moment when I should have invited him in, but I turned and blocked the door and said good-bye. Nobody in their right mind would let their parents in any of these places.

Days later, the FBI came to the "Dump" flashing badges, and I found myself stalling them the same way I'd stalled my Dad. Behind me was a living room full of dead joints in ashtrays, wayward baggies of dope. Apparently someone who had crashed here had been committing federal crimes with telephone codes. Once again I blocked the doorway, casting my shadow forward, telling them, "She's not here. I don't know where she is" until they went away. I seemed to have the ability to push people away with the very force of my aura.

When I think of those days, my life seems like a series of tunnels—lit pathways on dark streets, aisles between waitress tables, alleys behind apartment buildings, highways dim between headlights—and I was alone in each tunnel, surrounded by people rushing by. Eventually, I got my own place in a respectable neighborhood in a thin-walled apartment building where the local crimes consisted of raising Dobermans in the closet and beating your wife at four a.m. I invited my folks to dinner. My interactions with people became like the Texas two-step: While seeming to move toward attachment, I withdrew more deeply into solitude.

Finally, I made another geographic move. Again I went as far away as I could imagine going: this time, North Carolina. I began to see my place in my nuclear family as that of a distant planet, slung far out of gravity's orbit, cold and spinning. The freedom in my new life was heady. I began to reinvent myself on a foundation of days filled with exploration and possibility. I cut ties to the past and lived in the New World of Carolina.

Over the years I had been re-creating myself in the images of people I admired—picking up a cigarette trick from one, a trick of speech from another, a way of laughing, an ability to tease. Now all the parts of myself seemed to coalesce, recentering here in my new home. About six months after moving I got a call: my sister had disappeared.

I felt that familiar tug in my chest, the closing of my throat, the sinking of my spleen. Gravity, it seemed, was still working.

———

MY SISTER RETURNED UNSCATHED A FEW DAYS LATER. I realize this memory has come because of the strong sense that the Lumbee community excludes me, in a way that seems familiar, in the same way I exiled myself from my own family for years. As I cruise the darkening countryside of Robeson County, I know that tomorrow morning I must drive home, but I'm reluctant to leave without a closer connection to this haunted place, to the landscape and life here. The next day I return to the town of Pembroke, still hoping for a parade, then head toward the back roads, the long way home, on what will become a tour of town after town spangled with Christmas decorations. I drive, that most modern American form of exploration, one that insulates us with glass and white noise from what we see, as if the world were a kind of diorama.

Route 710 takes me past burning ditches and tobacco barns to Red Springs, a town with a surprising row of wedding cake Victorian houses. I remember my husband's grandmother lived here. And here is the sign for Flora Macdonald Academy, where his aunt went to school. I am driving past family history and it will no doubt remain a mystery. Both aunt and grandmother are gone. On the thinnest of connections, I begin to weave a story. I wonder what it would have been like to live here as a young woman in the early part of the century. I wonder if Sam's grandmother knew any Lumbee, heard the story of Henry Berry Lowrie— or for that matter, the story of Virginia Dare. I wonder if she was Lumbee herself. I wonder if her people were descended from the colonists. I remember her husband's first name was Samson, like the Bible strongman, but could it also have been a family name? A misspelled name from that old ship's roster? Like flame, imagination colors empty spaces.

More Christmas decorations, town by town, crossroads by crossroads. More low places, cypress knees, black water. A field with bales of cotton the size of semi trucks, wrapped in blue plastic. Doublewides, brick ranches, churches, and cottonfields mark lives here. The particular and unfamiliar keep me connected to what I see. As thin a connection as these windshield visions make, I am reluctant to return to the soulless highway, where history is counted in Pedro signs.

This is one of the places they say Virginia Dare's people ended up. Oral history, white man's writing, and tradition make the claim. Finally, here, Virginia Dare may live, but her story seems almost beside the point. The descendants of the people who lived, died, struggled, and fought here to survive now call themselves the Lumbee. They know who they are, and are tired of trying to prove it. It's tempting to think of the Lumbee ironically, to see them—the biggest Indian nation on the East Coast—as a Lost Tribe. But that's not how it is at all. The more I dig, the more I am reminded: I am the one who is a little lost.

All journeys bring one back to oneself. Perhaps who you are is the questions you ask. I remember now that Bruce Barton called out after me as I left his museum, his voice full of wry humor, as if to acknowledge that both of us understood all too well the limits of my search for Virginia Dare. "If you find her," he said, "you be sure and let me know!"

Chapter 10:

Back Home

> *[I]t is no longer adequate for a fieldworker to tell us*
> *what the native does day in and day out. We must now*
> *know what the native makes of all this as well. This is*
> *something of a Gordian knot for fieldworkers...*
>   —John Van Maanen, *Tales of the Field:*
>   *On Writing Ethnography*

SOLAR ECLIPSE. DECEMBER 25, 2000. I have punched a pinhole in a scrap of foil from the roasted turkey, brought out a business card, and lined them both up with the sun's rays. A tiny scale of light, like a clipped fingernail, beams on the card. But there's something off about it. It seems notched, not curved. I inspect the hole closely. The pinhole I have hastily made is shaped like an eclipse. I have made a lens which, rather than reading the true curve of light, reads its own shape.

———

EVERY SEARCH MUST END; this one has led me home to my own vision of my world; a place that repeats a dark pattern of loss and mystery as frequently as it seeks the light. I see now that this vision, if it were a painting, would show a wash of grief over the colors of the day. This is simply the eye with which I see the marvelous world.

Virginia Dare, born and baptized then lost to history, has been reinvented by the imagination for centuries, taking the form most congruent with the imaginer's vision. She is a goddess in white marble;

pure and virginal. She is an archetypal mother; a source, like a great river, of strength and blood for descendants of a convergence of two great peoples—the English and the Native Carolinian. She is the courage and intelligence of American womanhood. She is the romance of the wilderness; the hope of redemption; the light of Democracy in the New World; the loss of a child. I begin to see that for some, especially the "just folks" I talk to, Virginia is an emblem of grace—a blood sacrifice to atone for European sins against Native peoples. If we are all one, all descended from her image as English *and* Native American, then whatever divides us is inconsequential.

Or is it? My own instincts toward my subject have been these: to rescue Virginia from dusty obscurity; to tell the most true of the stories that are given by those obsessed with her; and to allow her story to push me to explore my own separations and losses. That so many have seen in Virginia Dare an emblem of America does not surprise me: The great migration of the English to North America made a matrix of hope and loss that still shapes experience for new immigrants and tenth-generation families alike. We hope for better futures, we migrate to new territory to find them. We explore; we separate; we move on. Our families become fractured in the process—regrouping and emerging in new forms.

Loss of the past is as much an emblem of our national psyche as hope. The losses of the Natives who held this land were the foundation stone for the invaders' success. The losses of African peoples—and those of more willing emigrants—were key to creating grotesque fortunes. The exploitation of great forests and natural resources ravaged the New World, and made dreams come true.

Whoever comes to these shores to start a new life, leaves an old life behind. We build new foundations on the ruins of our personal histories— just as in certain parts of Rome, apartment buildings rest their full weight on the tops of columns of buried temples.

Perhaps because I have burnt so many bridges, I feel I know how Eleanor Dare must have felt, waving good-bye to her father. Perhaps because I have started life over again so many times, eager and afraid, I feel a connection to Virginia, a child in the wilderness. And whatever losses I have known bring me closer to that moment in John White's life when the promise of the word "CROATOAN" carved in a tree became instead the nightmare mark of his life's great failure. Like a Jungian interpreting a dream, we can take every role offered by the story: the mother, the lost child, the grieved grandfather.

There are many more stories of mystery and loss that haunt my life. Virginia's silence compels me to speak a few of them.

———

IN 1984 I LEFT BEHIND A LIFE I no longer wanted and moved to North Carolina in search of some land and a new way to live. One of those I left behind was Abby. Abby had run away from home when she was fifteen; when I met her she was starting a new life after living on the streets. She was a dishwasher in the restaurant where I worked. In the summer of 1974 we rode cross-country to California in an old Mercedes full of hippies.

In Berkeley, three of us split off and hitched down the coast; in Big Sur, the two of us kept on going on our own. Abby and I hitched the long way home. We survived a speed demon who drove one hundred mph along the seaside cliffs of Route 101; we survived the L.A. police, guns drawn and pointing at our driver. In Arizona, a randy truck driver regaled us with Johnny Rodriguez songs, groped Abby in the sleeper cab, then dumped us by the side of the road at three a.m. in the middle of the desert. I remember hanging on that night, and the next day, in the rattlesnake-bitten Sonoran Desert; I remember squatting in a coffeeshop in Fort Worth, making my two dollars last till sunrise. I remember driving a stranger's car through Louisville rush hour, dawn breaking over Kentucky green hills. By the time we made it home, we were broke, exhausted, and hungry. I for one had lost my waitress shifts. I had to start over as a dishwasher.

I lost track of Abby when I started working office jobs. On a visit to the old neighborhood, I saw her sitting on a bar stool, her face beat up and swollen and her eyes defeated. She told me her boyfriend had a gun, had threatened to kill her. I could imagine this well; her boyfriend used to be mine. *Leave him,* I thought. I don't remember what I said. I left. I have never seen her again.

I have imagined the two of them many times since, an optimistic scenario in which he kicks all his habits and they move to a cabin on a lake. They spend their time fishing and hunting and raising dogs. I have not allowed myself to imagine anything else.

One day, long after I had given up thinking about Abby, I sat down to breakfast far away in the North Carolina mountains. I discovered that the poet sitting across from me had lived in my old neighborhood. The clues were unmistakable: dreadlocks and earring, he was reading the *Washington Post* and making political backtalk under his breath. Turned out he knew what became of some of my old friends. I began to list them for him: yes, he's still alive; no, she's moved on. When I asked him about Abby, I began to weep into my eggs. He had never heard of her.

Was she rescued or destroyed? I will never know—unless I try to find her.

THE MEMORY OF ABBY BRINGS TO MIND, one after another, all those in my life I have lost track of. Memory paints those faces in a wash of loss— they are people who I believed I could not rescue, and so abandoned. There are many stories I don't tell about my life. No one wants to hear them, least of all me. My myth about myself is that I have toughed it out, and things are good now. Things *are* good, but those untold stories haunt me, mostly because I have let them grow, in the half-shade of memory, into mutant things:

> *My first boss threatened to kill me.*
> *I hid in a cabin by Lake Erie for a month.*
> *Finally I left town in a snowstorm, in the backseat of a car so small I had to crouch to look out the windows.*

This story is true, in a way.

The truth of it is that I was eighteen, far from home, and afraid, and the life I had imagined for myself did not work out. The truth is also that I fell in love on the gorgeous polluted shores of Lake Erie. I kissed a man in an apple orchard and one night ate all the sweet corn I wanted, and nothing but sweet corn, and called it dinner. I lived in the attic of a German goldsmith, her husband, and their cats. I learned how to cash a paycheck; how to cook dinner for three. I watched the live birth of kittens for the first time. People were kind to me, or I would not have survived.

Then there's the story of my stepdaughter, who, just months after I lost the baby, went to live with her mother. Like that, she disappeared from my life. Stunned with loss and hurt, I kept telling myself, *She is fifteen, and that is a precarious age, full of painful furies.* Within six months, she had run away from her mother's house, escaping to the other side of the state in a borrowed station wagon. After a four-day vigil so frightening that all her parents ended up in the same room, she came home, and the next day dropped out of school. I spent two years sitting on my front stoop, chain-smoking, watching the smoke rise like a signal for help. The story I kept telling myself went something like this:

> *My darling red-headed girl, my only child, you are lost to me.*
> *The water is too deep, I cannot swim that far.*

I was wrong about that, of course.

There are other stories I could tell about my life, but they all are the same: they are all about loss, and grief, and hardship; they are all about leaving things behind, and moving on. They are history, and yet they live.

I know I am not the only one who clutches the past like a packet of letters from a secret lover. Sometimes, in a roomful of strangers, I try to imagine what their secret stories must be. I know they have them. At some point, I began to believe that even unspoken stories—or maybe especially those—carry their weight through generations. I still wonder what stories my grandparents never told.

MY PARENTS SURVIVED MOST OF THE TWENTIETH CENTURY in the New World. They stared poverty in the eye during the Great Depression. They listened to a planet-wide war on radios in the dark. They lived with the gaping knowledge of evil in the form of concentration camps and prejudice. They witnessed the gut-wrenching assassinations of the sixties; watched a national life seemingly overtaken by corrupt old men and terrorists in the seventies. They raised three children. The challenges they rose to were fearful; they faced them, as we all do, with courage borne in the knowledge that you cannot run from the times you live in. But what was it like to live in that way, in those times?

———

AUGUST 6, 1945. It's a month and six days since the wedding. They have been living that charmed, sweet life away from life, the honeymoon year, when the process of making a nest makes the world seem a safe place. Now they watch people spill out into the city street, cheering the great victory. The bombs fell on Hiroshima this morning.

They are horrified; they believe it might be the end of the world. An ungodly power has been unleashed on the earth. Who knows where it will lead?

Years later, a Hiroshima survivor tells my father a fact that strikes him to the core: The bombing was timed to occur at 8 a.m., so that all the people would be awake and out of doors. Farmers would be caring for livestock, children would be going to school, people would be going to work. It was timed so they would have no protection from radiation.

The pictures show, of course, that such protection would have made no difference. Buildings and people alike simply vaporized.

My father writes a poem:

> *. . . You are like the pilot who gave weather clearance for the drop,*
> *and later became mentally ill,*
> *for you suffer from a national neurosis,*
> *knowing what you would blot out of your mind:*
> *that on the morning of August 7, in the year 1945,*
> *the order was given to drop the bomb*
> *in the heart of a defenseless city . . .[1]*

———

MY FATHER TELLS ME HE TURNED DOWN METEOROLOGY TRAINING during the war, because his job would have been to give weather clearance for bombing. We both love the study of weather. We watch the Weather Channel for mysterious formations that will dump snow or ice or flood or drought on us in Biblical proportions. I can imagine my father giving reports to bombers—but *he* could not. I wonder sometimes where he got the courage to be so contrarian to his times, a peacenik in the midst of our most enthusiastic war.

"I don't keep a journal," my father says. "I wish I had."

"You still could," I say hopefully, as much giving myself advice as him.

"That's right," he says, sounding surprised.

"You could write down things you remember," I say.

This year I finally brought a tape recorder to a family gathering and began to ask questions. I learned my father's father, Elliot, must have been a wealthy man for a time before he died. "A millionaire?" "No," my father says. "But he made quite a lot of money." He'd sold all the furniture to the new *Chicago Tribune* building. He died soon after that, leaving his family a fortune in worthless bonds.

Hard times followed. My father remembers running to his mother when she fainted in the kitchen. As he tried to revive her, he heard her speak. "Oh Ellie," she said in her daze, "why did you have to leave me?" My father's eyes redden and he turns away.

I learn my father's Christian name was legally changed after his father died. I learn he had goose and plum pudding for Christmas dinner, and like me, lived with his grandmother for a time. I learn his mother was too proud to collect public assistance for widows, but neighbors made sure boxes of food were left on the back stoop. I learn he collected 5,700 pounds of newspaper to make the money for a Boy Scout trip to the Black Hills. I wonder if I have heard him right: *5,700 pounds*, piled up, day by day, in his wagon. In a shadow play of his father's losses, by the time he turned it all in, the bottom had fallen out of the paper market.

At a break in my questions, my father turns tables, playing a tape he made of his stepfather, "Uncle Pete." I remember Uncle Pete as a crusty, mustachioed cigar smoker whose voice broke in a mysterious immigrant accent. On this scratchy tape, barely discernible over crackle and hiss, Pete tells of eating stew on the farm where he worked as a young man back in Denmark, dipping his horn spoon into a common pot.

The spoon he chooses has delicate markings, striations of pink and blue and silver and black. With the rest, he dips and slurps, chewing a heel of black bread between mouthfuls of stew. When the pot is empty, the farm boys clean their spoons with a swipe of a finger, lay them on a timber ledge, and flies complete the cleaning. Again and again that last summer in Denmark, a fifteen-year-old boy comes in from the field, turns, and chooses: his only beautiful possession, a spoon in a rainbow of colors.

CHOWANOK. SPRING, 1610. *The copper must be burnt in pots over a fire, poured out on damp sand to cool, and pounded on a rock. The work has kept Virginia's fingers cut and blistered and sore for six years, and now they work like the claws of crabs over the ore.*

The boys have long since given up their hand-me-down britches. Sunburnt and peeling, in breechclouts of deer pelts, they are as dark and half-naked as the chief who brought them here, and keeps them here, as chattel. Still, the boys stay in good humor. Their small jokes make her smile from time to time. They work so quietly, she has almost forgotten how to speak. The one-armed Englishman makes her practice. He says they must remember; he says they are the only ones who survive.

"Queen Elizabeth," he tells her. "Sir Francis Drake. Sir Walter Raleigh."

She stares at the pink skin of his stump, remembering the day so many died.

He is teaching her the history of the world, from before she was born. She has never seen these things and does not believe in them. They make good stories to pass the time. A man wearing slippers crusted with pearls? He must be a great chief indeed. A cruel one, to be so rich and leave them here, forsaken.

The boys catch fish in their Indian weirs. The man grows melons in the summer. Village women bring them parched corn and a haunch of deer from time to time. They do not starve. The chief wants them to stay strong, and keep working. He wants his copper ornaments for trade; also, he is a little vain, like that Raleigh fellow.

Sometimes the Englishman shows her how to carve signs in the tender white skin beneath the barks of trees. She places her rough palms on the damp cambium and feels the words and letters press into them. A cross. A strange word: CROATOAN. The man carves trees in certain places where the Englishmen north of here might travel. He says he has sent word to the new English village across the broad river. He says they will rescue them soon. "Because we are English, too," the man has told her.

Sometimes Virginia dreams of swimming across the broad river he tells about. She wakes reaching out for rescuing arms. Today her mosquito bites itch and her hands bleed and she is feeling bitter. We are slaves, she wants to tell him. We are not the Queen of England.

IN FEBRUARY 1593, John White wrote an account of his last rescue attempt for Richard Hakluyt to publish. The account is full of "evils and unfortunate events." By the time his ships got to Virginia, "the season was so unfit & weather so foule," that they lost seven men and three anchors and most of their fresh water. In short, it was "lucklesse to many, as sinister to my selfe." White ends his tragic story by committing his colonists to "the merciful help of the Almighty."[2]

The last time he set foot on Roanoke was the day of his granddaughter's third birthday. Perhaps at that moment he thought of the ways of three-year-olds, how they take their world by storm, inventing it as they go. Perhaps he thought of his lost son, his wife, his daughter. Perhaps he thought of the tiny baby he baptized on that spot, so vulnerable to the world and its insults and terrors.

Three years later, when Virginia would have been six, he has given up on his kin. Perhaps he cannot bear to think of them. He has lost a fortune and an entire family. He is not heard from again in the published or unpublished papers of the English people.

What became of the proud, pearl-slipper-wearing Sir Walter Raleigh? Raleigh gave up on the colonists also, but not before sending a ship to search for them one last time. The ship returned with a boatload of sassafras and stories about how bad weather and lost anchors once more prevented a search of Croatoan. After Queen Elizabeth died, and King James took the throne, Raleigh spent considerable time in the Tower of London, suffering the new king's disfavor and writing history from his own point of view.

Raleigh had one last venture to the New World; this time he got to see it with his own eyes. He had always believed there was a gold mine in Guiana. King James, desperate for gold, and newly allied with Spain, allowed Raleigh out of the Tower to search for it, but stipulated that no conflicts with the Spanish would be tolerated.

Raleigh set out in 1617 to with his twenty-year-old son, Wat. Their voyage was as cursed as any other—with bad weather, fierce illness, political misadventure, and death. As his father lay sick in his cabin, Wat led a charge against a Spanish town, killed the governor, and was killed himself. The man who reported Wat's death to Raleigh then went to his cabin and committed suicide.

Raleigh's fate was sealed; King James would not forgive this disastrous turn of events. He grieved for his son, though, not his own sure fate, in his letter to his wife: "I never knew sorrow until now . . ."[3] Tried and beheaded, Raleigh left behind letters, poetry, and a *History of the World*. As was customary at the time, his wife received his preserved, severed head. She kept it with her until the day she died. The world would remember Sir Walter Raleigh—and his story—for a long time.

Epilogue

Searching for Virginia Dare

*The harvest is past, the summer is ended, and we are
not saved.*
                            —Jeremiah 8:20

*And here, poor fool! with all my love
I stand! no wiser than before.*
                            —Goethe, *Faust*

GREAT WOODE. KYLMORE, IRELAND. NOVEMBER, 1618. *John White sits in his
study by the peat fire, his drawings and papers around him in neat piles. Word
has come today of Sir Walter's demise. The messenger gave a full account: The
fine lord stood with honor, calmly denying the court's accusations. Then Sir
Walter confessed his most grievous sin—vanity. White remembers those pearl
slippers, that pomaded head, and almost smiles. Then his expression darkens.
All shreds of hope are gone for his family. Sir Walter was the only other man
alive who still had a stake in finding them, though his patent has long since
expired. Until this moment White has held on, bearing on faith what he knew
was against all odds, remembering how quick with words Sir Walter could be,
how convincing to men and women of power.*

*Now, one by one, the artist begins to feed his papers into the fire. From a
portfolio bound in leather he pulls drawings of the child—his catalog of Virginia,
marking each birthday. Here is a sketch of what she might be like now, in the
softness of middle age: matronly at thirty-one, mostly Indian, faintly English.
He has been as honest as he could be in his imaginings. After Powhatan, English*

men would have been scarce, if any survived at all. But Indians sometime spared the women and children of their enemies. Perhaps there was one who cared for her, one who was strong and kind.

White has painted his granddaughter, surviving, by giving up her Englishness. He has covered the strawberry cream skin with rough Croatoan garb—modified to conceal her fully, as is proper for a lady. He has strung her neck with pearls and shells, as a beloved Croatoan husband would do. He has made an ochre wash that reddens her cheeks and hands, and has smudged dark shadows of memory under her eyes.

Over the years, he has placed many babies at her back, held in that diagonal hold that seemed so peculiar when he first saw it. She would have married young, in the way of the Croatoan. In his last drawing, she has many grandchildren, one just a few months old, naked and laughing. Many times White has visited this vision of Virginia happy, surrounded by family, safe and warm. It has been enough.

The fire crackles noisily now, making lively ashes that swirl about the smoky lump of peat. A gale is blowing outside—as powerful a gale as ever blew a sailing vessel across the Atlantic and back again. Rain catches in the chimney pot, hurls a draft downward, flings sparks onto the hearth.

White opens another sheaf: Accounts of his age-old hopes for fortune. Page after page of numbers showing his losses, proving money is owed. Next, his journals. Diatribes against the Queen, against King James himself. Dangerous words. And finally, his will, showing his vast holdings in the New World. He has no such fortune to give—just an Irish house loaned by the grace of Sir Walter—and sacks of bills.

He feeds the fire, watches the ashes swirl and finally rise. He knows that if the story of Virginia will be told, it must be told by the survivors—and he is not one of them.

BLUE MEADOW FARM. JANUARY 2001. I have traveled hundreds of miles and studied scores of books and websites in search of Virginia Dare. I know more about Elizabethan history than I did, but not as much about archeology as I would like. I have read the personal letters of a Southern plantation lady and imagined myself dimly like her. I have accosted strangers across the state and asked them about white does.

I have walked among the Lumbee, lost and solitary as a stranger can be in a community where she does not belong. I have gone down blind alleys and left things undone: a canoe trip in the Great Dismal; a visit to the Buxton dig; a road trip to Brenau College. I have been forced to look at my own losses and how they shape me. As much as we wish to live in loveliness, it is tragedy and loss, bad weather and woe that make our stories stay with us. Loss lives like a shadow pattern, a template for disaster, in our minds.

When I imagine the fate of Virginia Dare now, I think of the story in *Catherwood*, a novel by Marly Youmans.[1] It is the tale of a colonist mother in upstate New York who gets lost with her one-year-old girl and wanders the forests of New England and Canada for an entire year, alternately wonderstruck with beauty and terrified, until the daughter dies of fever. The mother falls into a wild state of grief, carrying her daughter's charred bones on her back. It is a simple tale, with no claim to history, and though it has a tragic side, it ends in rescue by kind people.

This is the template for the story I choose to believe about Virginia Dare. If she or any of her kin survived more than a month or so, it required courage, and hard work, and the mercy of God or man. Perhaps they learned to love the landscape here, the deep forests, the Indian ways. Perhaps they came upon a lagoon of dark water, spangled with waterlilies, visited by white deer. Perhaps, torn by grief and war, separated into groups of twos and threes and fives, they wandered in that state of grace brought on by wilderness, bright water, cruel sun. Perhaps their bitterness knew no bounds.

No doubt all lost parents, and some lost children—that grief that turns a parent toward madness. Perhaps some conceived or fathered children whose English ways followed generations like a cheekbone's shadow, a cluster of words, or a chip from a porcelain teacup.

The Lost Ones are no different from the rest of us, yearning for brighter days, facing what life hands us, embellishing it with colors. Their story haunts because it lives in silence. Loss reminds us that life is a mystery; that death lurks beneath the surface of our cheerful days; that everything can change in an instant. In my grandmother's life, my stepdaughter's, and my own, that mystery opens and shifts, murmurs and drifts in the play of light, like the waters of Albemarle Sound.

A baby cries; her mother hushes her, rocks her in her arms until the heat and weight and tears settle on her breast. Where their bodies join a new thing forms: comfort and hope.

I begin to tell my story to the world.

Notes

Chapter 2

1. Excerpt from journal of Arthur Barlowe, first Roanoke Voyage, printed in David Beers Quinn, *The Roanoke Voyages*, 2 vols. (New York: Dover, 1991) 1:92.
2. Quinn, *Roanoke Voyages*, 1:82.
3. Ibid., 1:94.
4. Ibid., 1:96.
5. Ibid., 1:97.
6. Ibid., 1:95.
7. These illnesses may have included measles, smallpox, and the common cold, for which the Natives had no immune system defenses.
8. David Beers Quinn, *Roanoke Voyages* (New York: Dover, 1991), 2:378-79.
9. Ibid., 1:138.
10. Ibid., 2:518.
11. Ibid., 2:531.
12. "Rite of Baptism" from the *Book of Common Prayer*. 1559 Elizabethan edition.
13. Quinn, *Roanoke Voyages,* 2:537.

Chapter 3

1. http://www.law.ou.edu/hist/iroquois.html#funeral
2. Author and historian lebame houston spells her name without capital letters.
3. Donoh Hanks, ed., "The Lost Colony Souvenir and Program." (Manteo: Roanoke Island Historical Association, 1937), 20.
4. Hanks, "Lost Colony Souvenir Program," 1937. Virginia Dare wine is apparently still in production (see website: http://www.angelfire.com/tn/traderz/virginia.html). According to a website on grapes (http://www.newu.net/muscadine.html): "Scuppernong, the most famous type of muscadine, was used to make Virginia Dare Wine, the most popular wine in the United States prior to prohibition." Ian Frazier, in *On the Rez* (New York: Farrar, Straus, Giroux, 2000), claims a jug red Virginia Dare

vintage was a favorite at Casey's Golden Pheasant in Billings, Montana, once "the preeminent Indian bar in this country." 132-33.

Chapter 4

1. Excerpted in Hubert J. Davis, *The Great Dismal Swamp. Its History, Folklore, and Science*, rev. ed. (Murfreesboro, N.C.: Johnson Pub. Co., 1971).

2. Sir Thomas Moore, *A Ballad—The Lake of the Dismal Swamp*, in *The Great Dismal Swamp. Its History, Folklore, and Science*, rev. ed. Hubert J. Davis (Murfreesboro, N.C.: Johnson Pub. Co., 1971).

3. David Stick, *Fabulous Dare: The Story of Dare County, Past and Present* (Kitty Hawk, N.C.: Dare Press, 1949), 12.

4. John Lawson, *A New Voyage to Carolina*, ed. by Hugh Talmage Lefler. (Chapel Hill: UNC Press, 1967), 69.

5. Quinn, *Roanoke Voyages*, 2:811.

6. Quinn, *Roanoke Voyages*, 2:716.

7. Ivor Noel Hume, *The Virginia Adventure. Roanoke to James Towne. An Archaeological and Historical Odyssey* (Charlottesville and London: University Press of Virginia, 1994), 89.

8. http://www.arch.dcr.state.nc.us/ncarch/reporting/remains.htm

Chapter 5

1. F. Roy Johnson, *The Lost Colony in Fact and Legend* (Murfreesboro, N.C.: Johnson Pub. Co., 1983).

2. Robert W. White, *A Witness for Eleanor Dare* (San Francisco: Lexikos, 1991), 17.

3. Boyden Sparkes, "Writ on Rocke: Has America's First Murder Mystery Been Solved?" *The Saturday Evening Post*, April 26, 1941. Reprinted in full as Appendix C in *A Witness for Eleanor Dare*, by Robert W. White (San Francisco: Lexikos, 1991), 249-75.

4. Marc K. Stengel, "The Diffusionists Have Landed," *Atlantic Monthly* 285, no.1 (January 2000): 35.

Chapter 6

1. Cotten papers, Manuscript Collection at Wilson Library, UNC-Chapel Hill. SHC #2613.

2. Chicago diary, Cotten papers.

3. Letter written on March 23, 1986, Cotton papers.

4. According to Mentor L. Williams, in his introduction to an edition of *Indian*

Legends from Algic Researches by Henry Rowe Schoolcraft (East Lansing: MSU Press, 1956), in the first half of the nineteenth century there emerged a "rage for all things aboriginal." Schoolcraft published his Indian tales in 1839, which Longfellow adapted for his epic poem "Hiawatha" in 1855.

5. "The White Doe" (Philadelphia: J.B. Lippincott, 1901), 12. 2613 Cotton, Sallie S. Series 3 Vol. 14, Manuscript Collection at Wilson Library, UNC-Chapel Hill.

6. *NC Folklore 7*, Gertrude Allen Vaught, Alexander County, no. 7882, 486.

7. *NC Folklore 7*, unattributed, no. 7881, 486.

8. Movie typescript, 2613 Cotton, Sallie S. Series 3 Vol. 14, Manuscripts Collection at Wilson Library, UNC-Chapel Hill.

Chapter 7

1. *Virginian-Pilot*, 5 March 1996: B1.

2. Now published: E. Thomson Shields and Charles Ewen, eds., *Searching for the Roanoke Colonies* (Raleigh, NC: NC Division of History and Archives, 2004).

3. Shields does not use the term "Lost Colony" without quote marks; it is a nickname for the historical Roanoke colony of 1587.

4. Now published as a book: Michael Oberg, *Dominion and Civility: English Imperialism and Native America, 1585-1685*. (Ithaca, N.Y.: Cornell Univ. Press, 1999).

5. Richard Hakluyt, *Hakluyt's Voyages of the English* (London: George Bishop and Ralph Newberie, Deputies to Christopher Barker, Printer to the Queenes most excellent Majestie, 1589).

6. Hakluyt, *Hakluyt's Voyages*, 768.

Chapter 8

1. Anna Griffin, "Changing Times Bypass Hatcher of Robeson County," from series *The Terror of Robeson County*, 3 April 2001, Day 4.

2. One of the wonderful confusions about this geographic area in history is that John White had it wrong from the beginning: "Croatoan" was the name of the homeland of this tribe and its permanent village; "Hatteras" was the name of the people. John Lawson, however, understood that these were "Hatteras Indians."

3. Charlotte, N.C.: Associated Printing, 1967.

4. Adolph L. Dial and David K. Eliades, 2d ed. (Syracuse: Syracuse University Press, 1996).

5. Dial and Eliades, Only Land I Know, 6.

6. According to Douglas L. Rights, *The American Indian in North Carolina*. (Winston-Salem: John F. Blair, 1991), 7.

7. *The Lost Colony of Roanoke: Its Fate and Survival*. (New York: Knickerbocker Press, 1891). Reprinted from papers of the American Historical Association, Vol. V, 439-80.

8. Dial and Eliades, *Only Land I Know*, 13.

9. Stephen B. Weeks, "The Lost Colony of Roanoke, Its Fate and Survival." Exhibit CC in Indians of North Carolina, Letter from the Secretary of the Interior, Transmitting, In Response to a Senate Resolution of June 30, 1914, *A Report on the Condition and Tribal Rights of the Indians of Robeson and Adjoining Counties in North Carolina*, 63d Congress, 3d Session, S. Doc. 677. (Washington, D.C.: GPO, 1915), 65.

10. http://www.charweb.org/neighbors/na/lumbee1.htm. "Lumbee Tribal History"

11. Dial and Eliades, *Only Land I Know*, 49.

12. Ibid., 86-87.

13. Ibid., 67.

14. Exhibit B1. Petition of Croatan Indians. In *Indians of North Carolina, Letter from the Secretary of the Interior, Transmitting, In Response to a Senate Resolution of June 30, 1914, A Report on the Condition and Tribal Rights of the Indians of Robeson and Adjoining Counties in North Carolina*. 63d Congress, 3d Session, S. Doc. 677. (Washington, D.C.: GPO, 1915), 36.

15. Exhibit B2. Office Letter to Hon. J.W. Powell, January 7, 1889. In *Indians of North Carolina, Letter from the Secretary of the Interior, Transmitting, In Response to a Senate Resolution of June 30, 1914, A Report on the Condition and Tribal Rights of the Indians of Robeson and Adjoining Counties in North Carolina*. 63d Congress, 3d Session S. Doc. 677. (Washington, D.C.: GPO, 1915), 37.

16. Bureau of Indian Affairs website, visited 12/27/00: http://www.doi.gov/bia/bar/Indexr.htm

17. Pam Smith, "N.C. State University Sociolinguist Tracing Roots of Lumbee Language," NC State University News Release, November 23, 1998. Web source: http://www2.ncsu.edu/ncsu/univ_relations/releases/archives.html

18. *Indian by Birth: The Lumbee Dialect*, Prod. by N.C. State University with UNC-Pembroke's Museum of the Native American Resource Center and Department of Native American Studies, 30 min., videocassette.

Chapter 9

1. Stanley Knick, *Robeson Trails Archaeological Survey: Reconnaissance in Robeson County* (Pembroke, N.C.: Native American Resource Center, Pembroke State University, 1988).

2. *Strike at the Wind* Souvenir Program, Premiere Season, 1976. (Pembroke, N.C.: Robeson Historical Drama, Inc., 1976), 13.

3. Randolph Umberger, *Strike at the Wind*, Unpublished archival script, n.d., Archive Collection at the Institute of Outdoor Drama in Chapel Hill, 3-5.

4. Randolph Umberger, *Strike at the Wind*, Unpublished archival script, Archive Collection at the Institute of Outdoor Drama in Chapel Hill, 4-5.

5. Synge's play can be found in John Millington Synge, *The Tinker's Wedding, Riders to the Sea, and the Shadow of the Glen* (Dublin: Maunsel, 1911). To read Norment's

account look for *The Lowrie History: As Acted in Part by Henry Berry Lowrie, the Great North Carolina Bandit... a Complete History of the Modern Robber Band in the County of Robeson, and State of North Carolina.* (Wilmington, N.C.: Daily Journal Print, 1875).

6. Josephine Humphreys, *Nowhere Else on Earth* (New York: Penguin Putnam, 2000), 320-21.

7. Charlotte, N.C.: Associated Printing, 1967, 62.

8. Malinda M. Maynor, *Real Indian* (New York: Women Make Movies, 1996), film.

Chapter 10

1. From "The Harlot's Brow," by J. Elliott Corbett in *The Prophets on Main Street*, New ed. (Atlanta: John Knox, 1978), 165.

2. Quinn, *Roanoke Voyages*, 2:715-16.

3. Helen Hill Miller, *Captains from Devon: The Great Elizabethan Seafarers Who Won the Oceans for England* (Chapel Hill: Algonquin, 1985), 200.

Epilogue

1. (New York: Avon Books, 1996).

Afterword

The Search Continues

As I write, the British Museum is hosting an exhibit of John White's drawings, and Jamestown National Historical Park is gearing up for a season of 400th anniversary celebrations, complete with fireworks, pageants, and a visit from Queen Elizabeth II. New books have emerged on the subject of the first colonies and their relationship to the foundation set by the Roanoke adventures. It's a good time to be thinking about the origins of America.

Since the time the first edition of this book came out in 2002, I have had the good fortune to retrace the steps of my search, meet new people, and learn new things. I've actually tracked down Fred "Rosebud" Fearing and delighted in his Elizabeth City hospitality, which included a tour of downtown in a snazzy golf cart and a personal tour of his historical scrapbooks. I've visited Brenau University in Georgia and had the privilege of seeing the Eleanor Dare Stones—the ones in storage and the ones on display. I've visited the British Museum and had the great pleasure of leafing through John White's original watercolors, a portfolio still brilliant with the colors and the passion of his brush.

Phil Evans, a retired Park Service historian, kept me informed as archeologists in September 2006 undertook new research to search underwater for the remains of the Roanoke colonies. Just a week ago, my local newspaper reported that an amateur archeologist claims to have found crucial evidence confirming a completely new site for the village on Roanoke Island.

Here's to the mystery of Virginia Dare, wherever it may lead us!

Marjorie Hudson
Blue Meadow Farm
April, 2007

Selected Bibliography

Some of the following were source books for my research about Virginia Dare and the Lost Colony. Some of them are available only through research libraries. There's been a renewed interest in these subject, and many new books have been published that explore new areas of research, legend, and speculation. I've added a few new ones to the list.

—MH

To Learn More About Sallie Cotten

Sallie Southall Cotten. *The Legend of Virginia Dare*. Souvenir Edition. Manteo: Roanoke Island Historical Association, 1937.

William Stephenson. *Sallie Southall Cotten: A Woman's Life In North Carolina*. Greenville, N.C.: Pamlico Press, 1987.

To Learn More About Myths and Legends

Hubert J. Davis. *The Great Dismal Swamp. Its History, Folklore, and Science*. Rev. Ed. Murfreesburo, NC: Johnson Pub. Co., 1971.

F. Roy Johnson. *The Lost Colony in Fact and Legend*. Murfreesboro, NC: Johnson Pub. Co., 1983.

To Learn More About the Lumbee and Other Native Peoples of the Carolinas

Adolph L. Dial and David K. Eliades. *The Only Land I Know: A History of the Lumbee Indians*. Syracuse, NY: Syracuse Univ. Press, 1996.

John Lawson. *A New Voyage to Carolina.* Ed. by Hugh Talmage Lefler. Chapel Hill: UNC Press, 1967.

To Learn More About the Roanoke Voyages

Richard Hakluyt. *Hakluyt's Voyages of the English.* London: George Bishop and Ralph Newberie, Deputies to Christopher Barker, Printer to the Queenes most excellent Majestie, 1589.

Ivor Noel Hume. *The Virginia Adventure. Roanoke to James Towne. An Archaeological and Historical Odyssey.* Charlottesville and London: University Press of Virginia, 1994.

Phil Jones. *Ralegh's Pirate Colony in America. The Lost Settlement of Roanoke 1584-1590.* Charleston, S.C.: Tempus Publishing, Inc., 2001.

Karen Ordahl Kupperman. *Roanoke. The Abandoned Colony.* Savage, MD: Rowman & Littlefield Publishers, Inc., 1984.

Lee Miller. *Roanoke. Solving the Mystery of the Lost Colony.* New York, NY: Arcade Publishing, Inc., 2000.

Giles Milton. *Big Chief Elizabeth. The Adventures and Fate of the First English Colonists in America.* New York, NY: Picador USA, 2001.

William S. Powell. *Paradise Preserved.* Chapel Hill: UNC Press, 1965.

David Beers Quinn. *The Lost Colonists, Their Fortune and Probable Fate.* Raleigh, N.C.: Department of Cultural Resources, 1984.

David Beers Quinn. *The Roanoke Voyages. Vols. I & II.* New York: Dover, 1991.

E. Thomson Shields and Charles Ewen, eds., *Searching for the Roanoke Colonies.* Raleigh, NC: NC Division of History and Archives, 2004.

To See John White's Paintings and Theodor de Bry's Engravings of the New World

Kim Sloan. *A New World. England's First View of America.* London:

The British Museum Press, 2007.

Thomas Harriot. *A Briefe and True Report of the New Found Land of Virginia.* The complete 1590 edition with the 28 engravings by Theodor De Bry. New York, NY: Dover Publications, Inc., 1972.

To Learn More about the Eleanor Dare Stones

Robert W. White. *A Witness for Eleanor Dare.* San Francisco: Lexikos, 1991.

For Teachers

Roanoke Revisited: A Teacher's Manual. Conceived and developed by Lebame Houston, Wynne Dough, and volunteers. Manteo, N.C.: Fort Raleigh National Historic Site, Division of Visitor Services and Interpretation.

Web Links

Roanoke Colonies Research Office: http://www.ecu.edu/rcro/

Fort Raleigh National Historic Site: http://www.nps.gov/fora/

Native American Resource Center, UNC Pembroke: http://www.uncp.edu/nativemuseum/

Reading Group Guide

Questions for Discussion

1. Author Sheri Holman described *Searching for Virginia Dare* in this way: "Marjorie Hudson has beautifully united the personal and the poetic in her quest for the elusive Virginia Dare. By making this as much an autobiographical odyssey as a historical narrative, she challenges us to plumb our own dark interiors and seek out new shores of self."

Find passages of Hudson's poetic narrative. *What makes these sections "poetic"? How do these sections add to the narrative?* Find a few personal passages. *How do they work with the themes in Virginia Dare's historic story?*

2. Many people in the mid-Atlantic and Southern states grew up hearing the story of Virginia Dare and the Lost Colony. Some people have grown up knowing very little or nothing about it. *What did you learn as a child? Did you know there was a colony before Jamestown and Plymouth? Were you fascinated by the story? Why or why not?*

3. Native Americans feature prominently in the story of Virginia Dare. The author was intrigued by the history of the Lumbee people. *Do you know the history of a tribal people near where you live? Does your family or anyone you know claim Native heritage? Had you heard of the Lumbee before?*

4. There are three solar eclipses described in the book. Did you catch them all? Look for the "darkened sun" mentioned in the Thomas Hariot/ John White scene in Chapter 2. Then in a memoir section, at grandmother's house (Chapter 6), there is a brief image of tree leaves' shadows during an eclipse in the author's childhood. The third eclipse takes place in Chapter 10, in a brief section in which the author attempts to view the sun's shape using a pin hole in a piece of tin foil. *Read those three sections aloud. How does the idea of an eclipse relate to the themes in the book? How does the idea of an eclipse relate to the story of Virginia Dare?*

5. Prayer figures occasionally in the themes and musings of the book. John White reads from the *Book of Common Prayer* for the baptism ritual. Hudson makes a prayer of thanksgiving for finding her way in Greenville. An Iroquoian prayer for the souls of dead children is invoked. *How would prayer have been important to the colonists? How did Christian conversion affect the Lumbee Indians' fate and identity?* Hudson speculates that the images in Sallie Southall Cotten's epic poem were meant to be Christian symbols. *Do you see Christian themes in Cotten's life and poetry?*

6. "One of the best things about writing this book," Hudson says, "is sharing it with people and hearing the stories they tell back to me— about Virginia Dare, about grandmothers, gardens, growing up, hitchhiking, just about anything." *Did Hudson's experiences strike a chord in your life?* The book explores universal themes of missing people, losses, and times of upheaval. *Can you point to a time in your life of upheaval and change?*

7. Hudson explores the relationship between facts and myth in the book. *Did you learn any new facts that surprised you? Which Virginia Dare myth is your favorite? Do you think the Eleanor Dare Stones were a hoax? Why or why not?*

8. The author describes Virginia Dare's story as a family story, and as an American story. Families move, separate, and forget to pass information along. Children are lost, parents are lost. Those who remain, make things up. As a nation made up of people who come from somewhere else—or

who as Natives found their families and cultures devastated by European invasions—our collective memory is rooted in a pattern of loss and memory. *How does American history figure in to your family story? Are there any stories in the book—about Indians, for example, or immigration, that remind you of your own life or family?*

9. Hudson also claims that in America family stories are often lost or missing, yet they seem to remain alive inside the descendants. *Do you agree? If so, how might this be true in your own life?*

Author Comments

I WAS BORN IN 1953, in a small town in northern Illinois, the part with rolling hills and trees near the Wisconsin border. Our parsonage was next to the church on one side, the barber shop on the other, across from the courthouse and catty corner from the Piggly Wiggly. My life took a hard right turn when my family moved east to Washington, D.C., so my father, a minister, could study International Relations and peace. Eight years old, I missed my old life terribly. I remember tracing the highway on the map over my bed each night, following the route west with my finger, touching the places I once knew, lost and far from home. In Washington we grew up face to face with Cuban missile crisis scares, Kennedy assassinations, riots and anti-war demonstrations. My father took me to meet Martin Luther King in 1968; two days later he was assassinated. A sense of yearning for home, a sense of violent disconnection, a sense of the very personal pace of history—all these things had a great effect on me. Some of this personal history is reflected in *Searching for Virginia Dare*, a mosaic of history, fiction and memoir that turns on the story of first English child born in North America, who disappeared with her family shortly after birth. The book tracks Virginia's imagined steps through the coastal swamps and bays, following legends, tracking down weather studies and scholars, finding "lost tribes" and fanatics, and taking side trips and tangents into the 19th and 20th centuries. The book is my love letter to North Carolina—my adopted home for more than 20 years. I live on a farm in the rolling hills of the center of the state, not far from a small town with a courthouse and a church and a Piggly Wiggly (now defunct). I have worked most of my adult life as an editor and freelance writer, writing for nature magazines and editing everything from Southern fiction to law books. Now I'm working on a collection of short stories and a novel, both set in a mythical rural county in North Carolina.

You may download this book club guide and print it for your group's use at www.searchingforvirginiadare.com

Author Interview

Q & A with Marjorie Hudson

How is the story of Virginia Dare and the Lost Colony relevant to the 21st century?

I see the story of Virginia Dare and her people as a family story, looking for the intersections between large movements in history and personal tragedy. That kind of human story is always relevant to our lives, and especially during times of war or great social upheaval.

Why did you choose to weave memoir and fiction into the history of Virginia Dare and the Lost Colonists?

Perhaps it was because the more I traveled alone—and lost, much of the time, due to a terrible sense of direction—the more I gained access to memory and themes of loss in my own life. And the more I learned, the less certain I was of Virginia's fate—and the more I was cast back on imagination to find it. I began to write fiction scenes, following closely at first the journals of John White and others, then moving boldly into raw speculation.

I began to see that what people made of this story had a strange power their lives. Perhaps every journey of discovery leads one back to oneself. In my writing and notes, I stopped resisting the idea that my own journal entries were distracting or unimportant. I began to see how it was the way my mind worked—or anyone's mind—in the encounter with loss and mystery that was the most interesting part for me. So I threw everything in, made a jumble of it, then tried to make sense of it all. As a fiction writer, I knew that sometimes you have to take chances and let the material tell you how to shape it. So I wasn't tied to chronology and facts the way a historian might be. But my journalism background made me honor-bound to draw clear lines between fact and speculation.

In many ways this book defies categorization. How would you describe it?

It comes down to this: I started with history, hit a wall, turned to fiction, then opened up to memoir. Fortunately for me, in case anybody asks, I came across a term for this kind of cross-genre writing that combines fiction, memoir, history, or whatever. It's called the "mosaic form." Doesn't that have a ring to it? It calls up visions of saints on the walls of Roman cathedrals. It makes sense to me as a description of this book—many colors or shapes of material are fitted together with some kind of grout—in the case of this book, people say it's the friendly voice that holds it together. You could also see it like a jigsaw puzzle, but that doesn't sound anywhere as cool as "mosaic."

Although it is on one level a documentary, this book will not entirely make sense to someone who is looking for objective facts about history. It will make sense to those of us who are drawn to the subjective element in history – point of view and personal history—and who see the power such things have over their own journey.

You've stated that this story is about loss and transcending loss—could you explain?

As I worked, stories from my family and my own life that I had long since forgotten began to resurface. They all had to do with loss or a mystery of some kind.

Virginia Dare's story is a family story, and a quintessentially American story. Families move, separate, and forget to pass along information. Children are lost, parents are lost. Those who remain, make things up. As a nation made up of people who come from somewhere else—or who as Natives found their families and cultures devastated by European invasion—our collective memory is rooted in a pattern of loss and memory. That is why the story of Virginia Dare haunts me—it is our story too.

What set you on the trail of Virginia Dare?

I'd dimly heard of Virginia Dare in literature and history references after I moved to North Carolina, but I really had no idea of the weight and fascination the story would hold for me. The invitation to explore Virginia's story came in a letter one day from scholar, poet, and fiction writer Emily Herring Wilson, who is known for her work with women's history and biography. She suggested I write an essay for an anthology about North Carolina women in history, and the name Virginia Dare came up. I realized at once that I knew very little about Dare, and took that as a challenge. I knew the depth of my ignorance and was well aware that as a Yankee I had no right to claim this snip of Southern history. This, and my own tendency toward obsession, forced me to read everything on the subject I could lay my hands on. Pretty soon what I had written was too long. Emily said to keep writing, so I did.

Whom do you identify with most: Virginia, Eleanor, or Sallie Cotten?

Fiction writers "inhabit" characters as they write them. I think that's what happened for me with these historical figures. Virginia remains mysterious to me as she does to everyone else. From the record that remains, there is nothing from her point of view, so anything beyond a baby's consciousness must be completely invented. But we all have been infants. We all have been children. Some of us remember being abandoned or afraid. That's how I felt access to her character, but there was always a kind of shimmer around her true nature, as if she were a ghost that held a mirror, reflecting myself back to me, shielding her own essence in the play of light. Eleanor is a little easier to imagine or inhabit, because she was a grown woman in a new place—I've experienced some of that. Because I read Sallie's intimate life and daily journey in her own writing, I fell into "inhabiting" her very easily—though unexpectedly. I kept saying to myself, "Girl, what in the world do you have in common with a Southern plantation lady?"

You've said that since the first edition came out, you've received letters from people who responded to the story with great passion and personal identification.

That was a great surprise to me. At my very first reading, a friend brought me a pin from her grandmother's jewelry box, as a kind of legacy from her family story. Shortly after that, a young woman came up to me and said, "Your book is my *life*." Things like that kept happening wherever I went. I was amazed by that. I've also been very touched by letters from people who have illness or loss of a child in their families, and who say they have used reading the book aloud, or reading it at the shore, as a kind of healing. I do think books and stories can heal. They are an intimate view to the mind of another, which can be a kind of healing in itself.

You talk about the mystery of Virginia Dare—is there more to the mystery than her disappearance?

Lord, yes. There is the mystery of a great region and its Native people, and what life was like for them. There is the mystery of who all the colonists were, and whether their descendants survived as Native Americans. There is the mystery of family history—and the human obsession with the unknown, the missing, the family secret. This story has a strange power over people who know it, because it is a vessel, like those empty amphoras that were used to store anything and everything in the days of sailing ships. It holds the motion of the ship, the nature of the journey, as much as it might hold new wine.

People continue to come up with new theories about what happened to Virginia Dare, don't they?

Yes! One of the great fun things about touring with a book is you get to hear what people think. I've heard that Virginia's people migrated as far west as Chicago, based on a pattern of a conch shell found in certain graveyards. Another man told me he knew the location of Virginia Dare's grave. There are so many wonderful theories out there, I wish I could track them all down. Wonderful stories! It wouldn't surprise me at all if one or more of them were true. At the same time, there's been an absolute Renaissance in research and new literature on the subject. I'm learning new things all the time. It's tantalizing! What if we really do find her grave, her people, her descendants someday? It could happen. Technology is making it easier than it was. And as long as people are interested in the story, there will be funding for new research.

Okay, we have to ask: what's with the baobab tree in the first page of the book?

I always save this question to ask people at book clubs. Some of them guess right. I'll leave that a mystery! One clue—it's from very very far away.

Acknowledgments

Thanks to all the scholars and experts who took the time to talk with me about Virginia Dare, and to all the research libraries who provide materials for studies such as this one. The factual data in this volume can be attributed to their work, and the mistakes are all my own. Thanks to Headlands Center for the Arts, the North Carolina Arts Council, Creative Capital, Inc., North Carolina Humanities Council, the North Carolina Writers' Network, and the people at Press 53 for their support of this project. Thanks to the many readers of the earlier editions of this book who told me both stories of Virginia Dare and stories of their lives. Thanks to the many writers and researchers whose fascination with the topic has fed my own. Thanks also to my many teachers and mentors, especially Emily Herring Wilson, to my many writing groups who over the years have kept the flame alive, to the faculty, staff, and students of Warren Wilson College MFA Program, to my parents, who always have encouraged and supported my love of writing, and always, to Sam, who shoves the food under the door when I forget to eat while working away.

And last, thanks to the courageous and fascinating people who more than 400 years ago got this story rolling.

About the Author

Marjorie Hudson holds an MFA in Creative Writing from Warren Wilson College. She has worked as features editor of *National Parks* magazine, contributing editor of *American Land Forum*, and freelance contributor to many journals and magazines on the subjects of history, environment, and the arts. She has published poetry and fiction in *Yankee*, *Story*, and *West Branch*, among others, and essays in *North Carolina Literary Review*, *The Rambler*, *People's Civic Record*, and many other journals and publications, as well as in a forthcoming anthology *Wild in Our Breast for Centuries: Women and the Returning Realities of War.*

In 2000, Hudson was selected as Sarah Belk Gambrell Artist Educator of the Year, and in 2002 she was finalist for the Sherwood Anderson Foundation Prize. She was 2005 Artist in Residence at Headlands Center for the Arts in Sausalito, Ca., and recently two of her short stories were nominated for Pushcart Prizes and selected for Special Mention.

Hudson lives on a farm in Chatham County, North Carolina, with her husband, Sam, and various goats and dogs. *Searching for Virginia Dare* is her first book.

Readers can learn more about Hudson's appearances and publications on her website at www.searchingforvirginiadare.com.

About the Cover Artist

JOHN SAGARTZ was born and raised in the Midwest and he studied veterinary medicine at the University of Illinois and received DVM and M.S. degrees. He spent six years on active duty as an officer in the U.S. Army where he received specialty training in Veterinary pathology and became board-certified.

In 1992, after several years of work in veterinary practice and pathology research, he decided to make radical career change and began serious study in fine art. While continuing to work as a pathology consultant on a limited basis, he studied landscape painting under nationally acclaimed teachers such as Albert Handell, Doug Dawson, Lois Griffel, and Margaret Kessler.

In 1995, the lure of Italy took hold. He and his wife Christina, also an artist, traveled to Tuscany where they remained until 1997. They then moved to Rome for two more years and returned to the U.S. in 1999.

His work is representational. Although he admires the French and American Impressionists, he is reluctant to consider his style as purely impressionistic. His favorite media are pastels and oils. Italian landscapes and cityscapes take a prominent place in his body of work. Lately though, he has gravitated toward plein air painting. He and Christina travel extensively along the eastern seaboard in search of natural subjects. He has exhibited his work in numerous local and national juried shows. He has received many awards and his work appears in private and corporate collections. He and Christina work in their home studio in Winston-Salem, North Carolina.

A Proposal to My Readers

Virginia Dare Day:
A Day to Tell Family Stories
of Ancestry, Immigration, and Migration

Early in my research about Virginia Dare, I met a homeless man in Swansboro who told me his family story, a sad and possibly delusional tale of loss and disconnection. I listened to his story, heartsick and wondering, in the back of my mind, if he had come to me as a sort of Ancient Mariner, to claim my attention and give me a clue that would somehow be valuable to my search—a local tale, a bit of folklore, a family legend.

At the end of my Swansboro stay, as a reward for my sympathetic listening, "Willie" gave me a sweepstakes ticket with tiny spaces on it that I could fill in with my name and address in hopes of winning a grand prize: a North Carolina barbecue for 50 of my closest friends. I carried that coupon around with me for most of my journey—and still have it tucked in a box of notes. It seemed more important to me to keep it as a token of connection and hope than to actually fill out the tiny spaces and win the prize.

The promise in that small token reminded me a bit of the reunions on the farm in Virginia that my mother's family would hold in August on my grandmother's birthday. They also reminded me of my own wedding— a North Carolina barbecue if there ever was one—and other family events we've held on our farm over the years.

During scores of book signings and talks over the past five years, I've learned that the story of Virginia Dare sparks people to tell stories back. I've had the good fortune of hearing the family stories of Lumbee people, old-timers and newcomers to North Carolina, Alaskans, Midwesterners, "Yankees," and at least one Californian who stopped me on the docks at Manteo and asked me to sign a book, while sharing the story of her life. In our country, people are starved for someone to listen to their stories.

Back in Swansboro, my friend Willie had little to say on the subject of Virginia Dare, but his gift comes back to me now in the form of an idea—why not pick a day every year when people tell their family stories—the ones that they haven't got around to telling, and the ones that go back to ancestors, migrations, and immigrations? Why not call that day Virginia Dare Day? And why not celebrate it on Virginia's birthday, August 18, a marker for an end to the travels and heat of summer?

Virginia Dare Day could be a day when faraway children pick up the phone and call their parents or grandparents for a story from the past. It could be a gathering of family members in a town or county, or a gathering of neighbors who haven't yet met. It could be a barbecue for 50 people, a block party for hundreds, or a private conversation on the phone. It could be a time to tell stories within families and between families. It would be a time to answer the questions: Who are your people? How did they get here? And what are your family stories of failure and courage, true stories of struggle and hardship and survival?

For centuries, the story of Virginia Dare and her people and their fate has been lost to legend. Think of it! The first venture by English families into the New World—the first story that could be told in the language of those who followed and recorded history—has been virtually unknown to most Americans. The legend that remained glimmered like dust in a shaft of light in a darkened room. The real story is so much more vivid and alive. Because the venture was deemed a failure, and because its outcome remains unknown, we have not claimed this essential history and this magnificent myth.

We live in an age when millions of Americans of all backgrounds are seeking the full knowledge of their family trees; and millions of new American immigrants are hiding their stories of immigration and migration in attempts to assimilate. My own family tree reveals new branches all the time—connections in this generation to at least four continents as well as the discovery of a link to the Jamestown settlement.

Sallie Southall Cotten dreamed of ringing the Columbia Bell at the 1893 World's Fair in Chicago on Virginia Dare's birthday. Why not ring bells on that day nationwide and celebrate the stories that bind us together as Americans and the stories that will be lost unless they are spoken?

In the months to come, I will propose creation of a Virginia Dare Day to my legislators in North Carolina. I challenge you to join me, wherever you live, and to find a way to celebrate August 18 in your own very particular way.

Whereas, Virginia Dare was the first child of English parents born on American soil;

And

Whereas, the story of her family and her fate have been lost to history;

And

Whereas, Americans of all backgrounds can come together over the things we have in common in stories of ancestors, immigration, and migration;

And

Whereas, these stories of courage and failure, struggle and survival can inspire us;

And

Whereas, these stories will be lost if they are not told,

Be it therefore resolved that August 18, 2007, and every August 18 thereafter be proclaimed Virginia Dare Day—a day for Americans to tell family stories to each other and celebrate the struggles we have in common.

Marjorie Hudson
Blue Meadow Farm
May 2007

LaVergne, TN USA
15 October 2009
160912LV00003BA/4/A